FROM IMAGINATION TO REALITY

ALSO BY ABIOLA ABRAMS

BOOKS

*African Goddess Initiation: Sacred Rituals for Self-Love, Prosperity, and Joy**

Dare: A Novel

The Sacred Bombshell Handbook of Self-Love: The 11 Secrets of Feminine Power

CARD DECKS

African Goddess Affirmation Cards

*African Goddess Rising Oracle**

Sacred Bombshell Self-Love Journaling Cards

*Secrets of the Ancestors Oracle**

Womanfesting: Fertility Goddess Oracle

**Available from Hay House*

Please visit:

Hay House India: www.hayhouse.co.in
Hay House USA: www.hayhouse.com®
Hay House Australia: www.hayhouse.com.au
Hay House UK: www.hayhouse.co.uk

FROM IMAGINATION TO REALITY

Secret Manifestation Lessons and the Law of Assumption from Abdullah, Master Alchemist

ABIOLA ABRAMS

HAY HOUSE

HAY HOUSE INDIA
New Delhi • London • Sydney
Carlsbad, California • New York City

Hay House Publishers (India) Pvt Ltd
Muskaan Complex, Plot No. 3, B-2, Vasant Kunj, New Delhi – 110070, India

Hay House LLC, P.O. Box 5100, Carlsbad, CA 92018-5100, USA
Hay House UK Ltd, 1st Floor, Crawford Corner, 91-93 Baker Street, London W1U 6QQ, UK
Hay House Australia Publishing Pty Ltd, 18/36 Ralph St., Alexandria NSW 2015, Australia

Email: contact@hayhouse.co.in
Website: www.hayhouse.co.in

Cover design: Leah Jacobs-Gordon • Interior design: Bryn Starr Best

First published by Hay House India, 2025
10 9 8 7 6 5 4 3 2 1

ISBN 978-93-66119-23-6

Printed at Replika Press Pvt Ltd

MIX
Paper | Supporting responsible forestry
FSC www.fsc.org FSC™ C016779

Hay House is committed to a sustainable future for our business, our readers and our planet. This book is made from Forest Stewardship Council® certified paper.

CONTENTS

For my magical daughter, Amethyst-Ruby:

May your life be a remarkable journey, brimming with love, kindness, wisdom, riches, and endless possibilities. Within you lies the extraordinary power to manifest your dreams. It is the privilege of a lifetime that you chose me to be your mommy.

FOREWORD

Manifestation is not just a practice, it's a journey of the soul—an art of weaving the fabric of our dreams into the tapestry of reality. What Abiola Abrams has created within the pages of this book is more than just a book; it's a gateway to understanding the profound layers of your spiritual journey.

As a teacher of spiritual alchemy and manifestation for the last fifteen years, I've always believed in the transformative power of our thoughts and intentions. This book echoes a similar sentiment, delving deep into the Law of Assumption and the teachings and mentorship of Abdullah, the Master Alchemist. I'd heard of him before, but I never truly dove into his mystical wisdom.

As readers of this book, we're taken to a realm where our deepest desires are not just whims but potent seeds of our destiny, waiting to be nurtured. This book is a powerful reminder that true manifestation begins with intentional and consistent connection to Divine Consciousness.

Throughout my own journey over the years, I've witnessed the miraculous unfolding of intention into reality. I went from being a single mother living below the poverty line to creating a successful seven-figure business inspiring millions of people around the world to connect with the Universe and higher levels of consciousness. My life radically changed in direct proportion to how much inner work I was prepared to do. It's also important to note that despite the success and spiritual tools, there have still been trials and tribulations along the way. These challenges have been beautiful gifts and blessings because of the lessons they brought on how to transmute pain or problems into power.

By nurturing a thought into a tangible outcome, I've seen the Law of Attraction at work, harmonizing with the Law of Assumption, as beautifully elucidated in this book. The stories, exercises, and insights that Abiola shares are a testament to the infinite possibilities that await us when we align our imagination with unwavering belief in ourselves and our world.

This book is a beacon for those who seek to understand the mysteries of manifestation. It serves as a reminder that our reality is a reflection of our innermost thoughts and beliefs. As you turn each page, you'll be invited to explore the depths of your own consciousness and unlock the power of your imagination.

From Imagination to Reality is not just a read, it's an experience—a journey that will guide you from the realm of thought to the landscape of tangible reality. I am thrilled to introduce you to this profound work that aligns so perfectly with the teachings I hold so dear. May your journey through these pages be as transformative and enlightening as the practice of manifestation itself.

With love & gratitude,
Sarah Prout
co-founder of Dear UNIVERSE®, manifestation mentor, and best-selling author

PRELUDE

Greetings, Gorgeous.

If this book has found its way into your hands, it is no accident. God, Goddess, the Divine, the Most High, the Universe, the Ancestors, the Infinite Intelligence, the Great Mother, or (insert name of your choice) has conspired to bring you here. And life has been conspiring way before Abdullah was born to bring you this knowledge.

If you are here, you are seeking change—and you have decided to manifest your deepest desires. Whatever led you to these pages, you are exactly where you need to be. This book is a callout to your potential.

I once stood where you now stand, nerves growing around me like weeds. I was in deep self-doubt, where my big dreams felt like they were always just passing me by. I questioned my worth, my capabilities, and whether my desires had any room for me in this world. My hope was eclipsed by fear, and my faith was almost lost to skepticism.

But here's the powerful truth that I discovered: the same Divine Consciousness that designed galaxies, infused life into every blade of grass, and paints each sunrise is within me—and you. Yes, the same God, the same Source of All That Is, the same Cosmic Intelligence, wants us to manifest every desire we have.

I've experienced firsthand the power of conscious manifestation. Years ago, I accidentally manifested sleeping on a mattress in a dining room in LA, after I said that "all I needed was somewhere to lay my head." Since then, I've made leaps in my understanding of how to manifest intentionally. Today, I'm grateful to have manifested blessings such as my amazing daughter, a rewarding book deal with my dream team, a fun talk show pilot, and a GAP commercial. I've even manifested smaller but significant things, like finding a safety pin when I urgently needed one before a talk. Most recently, I manifested the perfect home. My journey shows that conscious manifestation makes a difference no matter the size of the desire or need.

It is your sacred duty to bring the life you imagine into existence. It's time for you to become who you were born to be.

Your desires are not whims. Your desires are a spiritual blueprint, waiting for your conscious realization to birth them into form. Your manifestations are not just your personal achievements. They are part of the grand evolution of life itself. Your desires are evolutionary.

Wake up. It's reaping season.

This book is your manual to unlock your divine potential within. You will discover the crazy synchronicities, wild coincidences, and effortless flow that become part of a life lived in harmony with the Divine.

Master Teacher Abdullah chose you and chose me. You are the artist and the masterpiece. What you are seeking is, in the most extraordinary way, seeking you too. Your desires are attracted to your spirit, waiting for you to realize them, to live them, and to become them.

No matter what you're experiencing, you are not alone. You are connected to every soul, past, present, and future, that has ever wanted something more. Consider a little girl in the Kalahari Desert who wishes on a shooting star, praying that her favorite giraffe might come closer to her dwelling, only to find it gracefully approaching the next morning. Or a young musician in rural Jamaica, manifesting his first gig. Or a double Dutch–loving little girl riding the New York City subway, manifesting writing this book for you one day, against all odds.

Across cultures, religions, time zones, and timelines, the intrinsic ability to create our reality unites us. It's a testament to our shared aspirations and the possibilities that lie ahead for all of us.

It is not a question of if but when. Your destiny is already written in the stars, encoded in the very DNA of the universe. But it's up to you to claim it.

Take a deep breath. Feel the energies of the countless possibilities swirling around you. Now, jump into these pages with the full might of your being, because within them lies the real secrets that convert dreams into reality.

Welcome to the first day of the rest of your magnificent life. Let's manifest some miracles together. These teachings have inspired me to dream bigger. You can manifest anything. And when I say anything, I mean anything. If I can do it, so can you.

May Abdullah's lessons also be your guide on your path to becoming the luckiest person in the world.

Put yourself on a new timeline.

Ase'! It is already done.

Love and magic,
Abiola

INTRODUCTION

Greetings Esteemed Reader, my name is Abdullah. I am the most famous mystic you have never heard of. I have influenced the spiritual teachers of your favorite spiritual teachers. You have picked up this book today so that you can enjoy a life beyond your dreams. My own personal story has largely fallen into the crevices of history, but through the power of the word my teachings remain.

— *Your Teacher*

In the land of ancient fires, where the cradle of humanity held its first dreams, perches the sacred Abuna Yemata Guh, an Ethiopian Orthodox church carved high into the side of a cliff. Abuna Yemata Guh was fashioned by human hands but clearly breathed into existence by Spirit.

The climb to this 4th-century church involves scaling sheer rock barefoot. Abuna Yemata is named after one of the "Nine Saints," a group of Syrian monks who spread Christianity in Ethiopia in the 5th and 6th centuries.

The early arrival of Islam in Ethiopia dates back to the 7th century, during the era of Prophet Muhammad. Instead of conquerors, refugees escaping persecution in Mecca introduced this faith. Hearing verses from the Qur'an, the compassionate Aksum king gave sanctuary to those fleeing.

The arrival of Judaism in Ethiopia is shrouded in legend and mystery. The Ethiopian Jews are also known as the

Beta Israel (House of Israel). The lineage of King Solomon of the Bible and the enchanting Queen of Sheba is said to have brought Judaism to Ethiopia. Another strand of their story links the Beta Israel to Jewish exiles who sought refuge after the fall of Jerusalem's First Temple, journeying first to Egypt, then Ethiopia. The sound of Jewish prayer might have graced Ethiopia as far back as the 10th century b.c.

When the Abrahamic faiths entered Ethiopia, they were integrated into a rich spiritual and philosophical heritage. Ethiopian indigenous religions provided fertile soil for the seeds of mysticism and esoteric interpretations within Islam, Judaism, and Christianity to flourish.

When I told a friend that I was writing the manifesting secrets of an Ethiopian mystic, she asked if there is "conjure" in Ethiopia. The term *conjure* typically refers to a system of personal magic, healing, and spirituality with roots in West Africa that was first practiced in America by enslaved Africans. The practices often include the use of herbs, roots, and other natural elements, along with Psalms, invocations, and spiritual rituals.

While the term conjure isn't traditionally used in Ethiopian culture, Ethiopia has a rich history of indigenous spiritual practices, many of which include similar elements. For example, certain Ethiopian traditions incorporate the use of herbs and natural elements for healing and protection, and rituals or ceremonies may be conducted to contact spiritual entities or ancestral spirits.

Alchemy in Ethiopia has been closely associated with Coptic Christianity, local mysticism, and indigenous practices. One of the most iconic texts associated with Ethiopian spiritual alchemy is the "Wisdom of Solomon," which delves into alchemical principles of divine knowledge, metaphysical truths, Biblical insight, and the transformation of the soul.

Many ethnic groups in Ethiopia practice elements of alchemy. Sufism, the mystical dimension of Islam, has a significant presence in Ethiopia. In Ethiopian Sufism, the practice of dhikr, or the remembrance of God, is about manifesting divine qualities within. This tradition teaches that by purifying your inner self, you create better external life circumstances. Sound familiar?

Transformation, a core theme of alchemy, permeates Ethiopian folklore, religious texts, local healers and medicine, and traditional practices. In this unique environment, ancient Ethiopian scholars, storytellers, and mystics were already exploring timeless truths, often pre-echoing some of the principles later found in the New Thought movement.

Magical manifesting traditions in Ethiopia include:

- In the Oromo culture spiritual leaders perform rituals with herbs and minerals to transform negative energies into positive ones.
- The agricultural Gurage people see the natural world as a reflection of divine truth, similar to the Law of Attraction's focus on reciprocal energy exchange.
- In Tigray's northern region, the ancient Tsamai belief system involves aligning earthly actions with spiritual intentions.
- The Hamar people's beliefs align with the view of unseen spiritual forces influencing the material world.
- The Konso people embodied the mystical idea of cause and effect or "as above, so below."

- The vision and faith of the Afar people, despite their harsh living conditions in the desert regions, aligns with the Law of Assumption's focus on positive expectation.

And these are just a few examples. This is the land of power, faith, and philosophy that birthed the mystic known only as Abdullah: visionary, seer, scholar, alchemist, and spiritual teacher.

Enter Abdullah

I willed it so to be, I still will it so to be, and I will will it so to be until that which I have willed is perfectly expressed.

— *Abdullah*

Thought leader Abdullah was a Black Ethiopian Jewish rabbi with a Muslim name who taught spiritual lessons in early 20th-century New York City. Turbaned, tall, and majestic, with beautiful jet-black skin, this was not a man who faded into the background. You may never have heard his name, but you have heard his transformational spiritual lessons that still reverberate today.

Abdullah was most likely born in the 1840s, and he lived to be over 100 years old. According to his secretary, he returned to Ethiopia to die in 1957, having lived in Oxford and New York City, among other places. Prolific author Joseph Murphy believed him to be from Israel, so perhaps he was able to visit that region too. Abdullah lived at the prestigious Morgenthau mansion at 30 West 72nd Street, off Central Park West in Manhattan, just crosstown from where I attended middle school and high school on East 83rd Street.

Abdullah's known students included New Thought leaders Neville Goddard (known simply as Neville), Dr. Joseph Murphy, Winifred MacCardell Flood, and possibly John McDonald and Walter C. Lanyon. Neville said that Abdullah counseled luminaries: "Scientists, doctors, lawyers, bankers, from every walk of life [sought] an audience with old Abdullah, and everyone who came thought themselves honored to be admitted to his home and to receive an interview. If he was ever invited out, and he was, he was always the honored guest."[1] Rabbis would also come to study with him.[2] Abdullah's building was known for its spiritual empowerment classes. Neville also told friends and acquaintances like Freedom Barry, Lindell Warden, Margaret Ruth Broome, and Israel Regardie about his experience with the "brilliant, wonderful gentleman"[3] Abdullah, called an "eccentric" and "giant Ethiopian rabbi" by Regardie.[4]

Yet there are those today who doubt that Abdullah existed. It's not easy for some people to picture a Black man in Jim Crow America commanding life as Abdullah did. I will not be investigating Abdullah's realness here or trying to prove he existed—because he did. To be honest with you, I find the mental gymnastics people have gone through on this topic extremely offensive. One author even courageously confessed, "I had difficulty believing Abdullah was real at first because he seemed so 'white' to me, but that's how ignorant of history I was."[5]

Perhaps it's because my own father is a cranky, old, wise Black professor, clergyman, and spiritual teacher from another country that I don't get the vibe of imaginary, mysterious guru or "magical negro" from descriptions of Abdullah. I feel him as a knowledgeable, sage, practical, life-changing practitioner. Maybe it's because I come from cultures that prize oral literature, but I feel that I have known several Abdullahs in my life.

Abdullah didn't leave much of a paper trail. But he was real. In fact, I feel his energy all the time, and you will too. For every doubter, there are groups of passionate seekers and believers on Reddit, Facebook, and other forums who have also been positively obsessed with and possessed by the wisdom of Abdullah. The purpose of this book is to share his transformational lessons. That is my divine assignment and sacred calling.

You have a duty to use manifestation to create your most beautiful life. You are an alchemist with the power to birth worlds. Your manifestations expand consciousness for all of us. Anything you see in front of you now first existed in someone's imagination. You are part of evolution. We all are.

When the ancestral metaphysicians want to get your attention, they make it happen. Take the fact that you are holding this book. It is not by accident. In fact, if you think on how you came upon these teachings or even how you found me, the path is quite magical, isn't it?

About 10 years or so ago, I decided to hermitize myself in my parents' home for a few weeks to heal after a particularly horrific breakup. Every morning I went out on their porch to journal and would say hello to Steve, the mail carrier. I don't recall how the conversations on manifesting started, but my mother's mailman started to tell me about Neville Goddard. Tell is the wrong word. Steve started to implore and insist urgently that I read Neville.

Around the same time, my mentor in my head, Dr. Wayne Dyer, started singing the gospel of Neville and published *Wishes Fulfilled* based on his teachings. I listened to Dr. Dyer Mondays at 4 P.M. on Hay House Radio. At that time I was teaching The Secret and affirmations and was already a student of Florence Scovel Shinn and Abraham Hicks. After college I was blessed to intern at CNBC's self-help talk show *Alive and Wellness,* which featured Louise Hay's work, and rode the subway reading Iyanla Vanzant's first book. So I thought I knew all I needed to know and assumed that all of the "New Thought" leaders of Shinn's era were saying the same thing.

Growing up, my dad had quite the library of spiritual books and a subscription to an "odd" esoteric publication called the *Rosicrucian Digest,* which had a children's section. My sister and I made vision boards as kids, although we didn't call them that. So none of this was strange to me. I just assumed I had all the information.

When I finally went back home to Harlem and started to read about Neville, I was shocked to discover that he was born in Barbados. This initially turned me off. My great-granddad David was Bajan (Barbadian), and I knew that any European from Barbados or Guyana (where the rest of my family is from) may have had direct ties to those who colonized or enslaved my ancestors—and Goddard's ancestors were known for being good at business.[6] In fact, Neville was born on a sugar plantation in a planter's family; my enslaved family worked the cane plantations. He even mentions his brother Cecil moving to Demerara, Guyana, presumably to sell.

On a deeper dive, I was electrified to learn about and "meet" Abdullah, the Black man who was Neville's mentor and spiritual teacher.

"He was as black as the ace of spades, my old friend Abdullah, with his turbaned head," writes Neville. Yet by all accounts Abdullah lived life on his own terms during the age of segregation in the United States.

Charismatic spiritual teacher Abdullah was known for his bold teaching methods and his ability to convey complex metaphysical concepts in simple, easily workable terms. For example, Abdullah belched to approximate and teach the correct sound in Hebrew יהוה of the name of God. Abdullah was also a master of esoteric knowledge, and he had psychic abilities. He taught Christian principles with a deep understanding of the Old and New Testaments of the Bible as well as the Kabbalah, and incorporated these teachings into his own spiritual philosophy. Strict with his students, Abdullah demanded devotion, discipline, and dedication.

Take it from Neville: "When I first met my friend Abdullah back in 1931, I entered a room where he was speaking and when the speech was ended, he came over, extended his hand and said: 'Neville, you are six months late.' I had never seen the man before, so I said: 'I am six months late? How do you know me?' and he replied: 'The Brothers told me that you were coming, and you are six months late.'" The Brothers refer to Elohim, the Divine, God, or gods.

Abdullah means "servant of God" in Arabic. The name Abdullah, typically associated with Islam, might appear among Jewish Ethiopians for several reasons. As an Ethiopian friend explained to me, this cross-cultural naming is not as uncommon there as it might be in other regions. The name could come from conversion or interfaith marriage, where one parent is Jewish and the other is Muslim. In areas with a long history of folks coexisting within different religious communities, names from one tradition become popular in another. Some might adopt a name due to its association with a respected figure, regardless of religion. Some Jewish communities in Ethiopia were in hiding for centuries due to fear of persecution. In such areas, adopting names that were common among the majority could be a strategy to protect their identity.

In Ethiopia, holy men who transcend religion are known as dabteras. Neville described Abdullah as a rabbi who was also a master teacher of Christianity. Ethiopian mysticism emphasizes a direct and personal relationship with God through the use of meditation, prayer, and other practices. Ethiopian mysticism is influenced by a variety of traditions, including their indigenous lineage religions, Judaism, Islam, and Christianity. Some of their key tenets across the board include: oneness/the interconnectedness of all things, alchemy, meditation, the power of community, and the use of symbols and ritual. Ethiopian tradition teaches that the Ark of the Covenant, which contains the tablets of the Ten Commandments, is preserved in the ancient city of Aksum.

There is some overlap between Ethiopian mysticism and Kabbalah. Both traditions emphasize the importance of seeking spiritual knowledge and understanding, and both view the world as being infused with divine energy. Both traditions use forms of meditation and visualization to connect with this divine energy and deepen spiritual understanding.

In Kabbalistic thought, our physical world is seen as an extension of our spiritual world, and our thoughts and actions have the power to influence the spiritual forces that shape reality. Kabbalistic teachings emphasize the importance of positive thinking and the visualization of positive outcomes for manifesting.

There is also overlap between some kinds of Ethiopian mysticism and ancient Kemetic thought. The Kingdom of Aksum, an ancient civilization in what is now northern Ethiopia and Eritrea, had interactions with ancient Egypt, and may have shared some aspects of Kemetic philosophy and spirituality.

The mother and father of the modern mainstream self-help spiritual movements, Louise Hay and Wayne Dyer, were connected to and directly influenced by Abdullah's most famous students, New Thought movement pioneers Neville Goddard and Joseph Murphy.

Goddard and Murphy were both so moved by the teachings of this Black man in the early 20th century that they mentioned him in their work. Undoubtedly many others who did not cite him were also influenced by Abdullah. The most documentation of Abdullah we have comes from Neville's lectures and books. We know that Abdullah taught Neville kabbalism, mysticism, New Thought and Biblical lessons, and conscious creation. So, I will share those lessons from Neville's works that we know originated with Abdullah. I will also share from the relevant teachings of Abdullah heirs, disciples, and rumored disciples, including authors and spiritual teachers: Dr. Murphy, Walter C. Lanyon, Winnie MacCardell Flood, Freedom Barry, Lindell Warden, Margaret Ruth Broome, John McDonald, and more. Neville's direct students and those influenced by Neville also included people like popular Black Science of Living minister Reverend Ike, spiritual master teacher Bob Proctor, Carlos Castaneda, Rhonda Byrne, and Catherine Ponder.

Want to manifest an empowered life?

Abdullah left us alchemical wisdom and gifts to co-create our desires. His most famous pupils not only passed the wisdom onto us, but they also used these teachings to build their dream lives. Neville was a prolific businessman who manifested his wife; Dr. Murphy manifested his dream mansion, and they both manifested being renowned author-teachers with wealth and fame.

If Abdullah has remained hidden and mysterious, I trust and believe that this is how he manifested things to be. You will find that as elusive as he is historically, he has a persistent and enduring energy. Once I learned about him, his spirit would not leave me alone.

How to Use This Book

Ready?

You now hold the keys to unlock your manifesting potential and create a life beyond your wildest imaginings. As you immerse yourself in this book, allow yourself to release old beliefs and programming. Embrace the idea that you have the power to create a life beyond your imagination. Approach these teachings with a sense of curiosity, as if you are embarking on a grand adventure. You are!

You can experience this book and Abdullah's lessons in a few different ways. The most powerful way is to read it straight through, allowing the teachings to build on each other. You can also read section by section, taking time to reflect and practice the concepts before moving on. Another approach is to let your intuition guide you on the perfect order of the mysteries and processes.

This is not so much a book you read as it is a book you do. You will find the aligned approach that supports your manifesting and growth.

SCROLLS

Trust in your innate power to create the life you desire. Watch as everything seems to conspire to bring your dreams into reality. Abdullah's spiritual laws (mysteries) allow us to go from imagination to reality.

DECREES

Abdullah believed in the power of affirmative words, called "autosuggestions" at the time. He repeated the unity prayer before his classes and had his students commit to memory excerpts from the Bible to use as affirmations. Abdullah used to chant the following autosuggestion:

> I willed it so to be, I still will it so to be, and I will will it so to be until that which I have willed is perfectly expressed. I haven't forgotten what I willed. I willed it so to be. I still will it so to be. I will continue to will it so to be until what I have willed is perfectly expressed. So I will assume that I am that which I want to be. I'm still assuming that I am it. I will continue to assume that I am it until what I have and still am assuming is externalized and is expressed.[7]

Phew! Abdullah's extended affirmation is a decree on persistence and holding to your vision. Growing up, I was very inspired by the work of old-school motivational author Og Mandino, who shared extended affirmative statements in his work. In the vein of Abdullah's proclamation, and the teachings of Og Mandino, each chapter has a decree for you to read to yourself. The decrees are affirmative statements to reprogram your mind. Repetition is extremely powerful for rewriting thoughts. You may choose to read each decree for 30 days, 3 times a day if you really want to make impact.

JOURNAL QUESTIONS AND EXERCISES

Self-reflection is a powerful tool for creating what you want. Take time to reflect on your current beliefs, desires, and patterns. Throughout this book, you will also encounter thought-provoking journal questions designed to deepen your understanding and accelerate your manifestations. Use the prompts to journal your thoughts, fears, and desires as you progress through the book. Set aside dedicated time for this work.

BONUS: THE PROCESSES

At the end of this book I share five of Abdullah's manifesting processes. These processes help you to align your energy and intentions with your desired manifestations. Each process is designed to engage your mind, emotions, and actions in a synergistic way. You may choose to do any of the processes at any time. Follow them with an open heart and a willingness to experiment and explore, even if you don't fully understand them right away. Feel free to adapt them to suit your truth.

YOUR TEACHER

Throughout the book, you will notice quotes from "Your Teacher." To create a distinction between Abdullah's quotes and the channeled wisdom that I received from him, Abdullah's quotes are signed as "Abdullah" while the channeled excerpts are attributed to "Your Teacher."

PART I:

THE FOUNDATION

I picked up this garment
ninety-odd years ago in Ethiopia.

— Abdullah

Dear Esteemed Reader,

You stand at the threshold of an extraordinary path, one that has the potential to reshape your understanding of what it means to be a conscious creator—and your world. As you embark on this adventure, you shall first lay the groundwork in "The Foundation." The Foundation is where you will establish the bedrock principles that underpin the art of conscious creation.

I invite you to begin this pilgrimage of self-discovery and prepare to reawaken your own creative gifts.

May you come to know the operant power that resides within you, and may you use it to bring forth a world that reflects your innermost desires.

With profound respect and heartfelt blessings,

Your Teacher

Welcome to "The Foundation," your starting point into the world of manifesting. In this section, we will explore the essential concepts of conscious creation. Here, you will gain an understanding of the principles that underpin the manifesting process, providing you with the tools you need to harness the power of your imagination to bring forth your deepest desires.

THE ABDULLAH PARADIGM: I AM

Have you ever felt that there's a powerful part of you that's more than just your name, job, or interests? This is what Neville called the "I AM" consciousness. It's like the superhero version of ourselves, always present, always powerful, even if we don't always notice it.

This paradigm captures a truth that goes beyond self-affirmation. Your "I AM" consciousness is the manifestation of the divine within you.

This phrase draws from Old Testament Biblical scripture relaying the moment when God declares to Moses, "I AM THAT I AM." It isn't just a declaration of God's identity; it's an invitation to recognize that this divine essence, this omnipotent energy, is in each of us. When we say, "I AM," we're invoking the omnipresent divine energy that shapes everything.

The Abdullah Paradigm challenges us to deliberately embody this "I AM" consciousness. This is more than a method—or even a mindset. It's about aligning our desires, dreams, and aspirations with the eternal and limitless potential of the divine force within.

The Abdullah Paradigm invites us into a deeper understanding of manifestation. It's like the main ingredient in the recipe. If we understand this, all other teachings and lessons make more sense. It's about knowing that deep inside, we have the power to create our world. And at its core is that special feeling of "I AM" reminding us that we're way more powerful than we think.

Manifestation through "I AM" Consciousness

Imagine standing at the edge of a beautiful forest. One path leads to a journey of constant yearning and hoping with signs labeled "I want." Another path has a golden inscription reading "I AM," leading toward a journey of realization and fulfillment. Our choice between these paths is how we navigate manifestation.

For most of us, "I want" is familiar. Phrases like "I want to succeed," "I want love," or "I want peace" are almost second nature. But these carry an undertone of lack. "Want" says that what we seek is distant, removed, or unattainable.

Now, consider the power of "I AM." When we declare "I AM successful," "I AM love," or "I AM peace," there's a seismic shift in perspective. You're no longer outside of your dreams. You stand at their very core. "I AM" is the bridge that takes you from wishing it to living it.

Exercise: The "I AM" Meditation Process

Purpose: To empower your manifestations by entering the void state.

> Dwell upon just being by saying, "I AM," "I AM," "I AM," to yourself. Continue to declare to yourself that you just are. Do not condition this declaration, just continue to FEEL yourself to be and without warning you will find yourself

> slipping the anchor that tied you to the shallow of your problems and moving out into the deep.
>
> This is usually accompanied with the feeling of expansion. You will FEEL yourself expand as though you were actually growing. Don't be afraid, for courage is necessary. You are not going to die from your former limitations, but they are going to die as you move away from them, for they live only in your consciousness. In this deep or expanded consciousness you will find in yourself a force that you had never dreamed of before.[1]

That's a powerful quote from Neville about the importance of simply being and dwelling in the state of "I AM."

In the teachings of Abdullah, we uncover a world where our inner thoughts and beliefs hold the keys to shaping our outer reality. But beyond the power of the conscious mind, there is an even deeper level of awareness. This is the realm of God consciousness, a space where we connect with the divine spark within us, the eternal part of ourselves that is interconnected with the Divine. Here is where we can unlock the ultimate potential to manifest our dreams and live our most fulfilling lives. One of the most powerful ways to access this state of being is through "I AM" meditation.

The "I AM" meditation technique is a direct channel to your innate God consciousness. By repeatedly affirming "I AM," you align yourself with the power of creation.

As you delve into the "I AM" meditation, you'll experience a sense of expansion and connection that transcends your everyday self. You'll find yourself moving beyond limitations. This is the state of pure being, where the power to manifest your dream life becomes a reality. This will help you navigate your alignment with God consciousness.

The practice of the "I AM" meditation can reshape your understanding of yourself and the world around you.

What to do:

1. **Find a quiet and comfortable space** where you can sit or lie down without being disturbed. You want to be relaxed but alert.
2. **Close your eyes.** Take a few deep, slow breaths. As you exhale, release any tension or stress. Allow your muscles to relax, and let go of any worries.
3. **Focus on your breath.** Notice the rise and fall of your chest as you inhale and exhale. Allow your breathing to be natural and effortless.
4. **Begin repeating "I AM" silently.** Repeat the words "I AM" in your mind. You can say it aloud if you prefer. Say the words slowly and with intention. As you repeat "I AM," let go of any other thoughts, judgments, or distractions that arise.
5. **Stay present and connected.** Try to focus only on the words "I AM" without adding any other thoughts, feelings, or qualifiers. If your mind starts to wander, gently bring your attention back to "I AM."
6. **As you meditate, you may notice that you are experiencing certain sensations, emotions, or insights.** Observe them without judgment and allow them to come and go. Stay anchored in the state of "I AM," simply being and observing.
7. **Gradually end the meditation.** After about 10 to 15 minutes (or longer if you prefer), gradually bring your meditation to a close. Slowly

deepen your breath, and become aware of your surroundings. Open your eyes and feel gratitude for the experience.

By practicing the "I AM" meditation regularly, you can connect with your innate God consciousness, cultivate a deeper sense of self-awareness, and tap into your inner power to manifest your dream life.

Exercises: Deepening Your Practice with "I AM"

When you embrace the "I AM" consciousness, manifestation becomes more about reclaiming the magic already inside you. This makes every step you take intentional, focused, and powerful. When you embody the "I AM" presence, you don't just bring your desires to life, you become them.

Here are some practices to align with your "I AM" essence:

- **"I AM" Role Play:** Spend a day embodying a specific "I AM" statement. If you choose "I AM confident," for example, dress, speak, and act in ways that exude confidence. Engage in activities you'd typically shy away from and note how this shift in identity alters your experiences.
- **Interactive "I AM" Board:** Design a tactile board or space in your home that's dedicated to an "I AM" that you are consciously manifesting. Incorporate textures, materials, colors, and objects that represent your statement or affirmation. Touch, rearrange, and interact with this board daily to feel and reinforce your chosen state of being.

- **"I AM" Dialogue:** Temporarily imagine your "I AM" essence (like "I AM courage" or "I AM love") as a separate entity. Ask it questions, seek guidance, and listen for answers.
- **"I AM" Sound Bath:** Curate a playlist or collection of sounds that resonate with a your chosen "I AM" statement. For "I AM peaceful," for example, you might include gentle rain, soft chimes, or tranquil melodies. Let the sounds amplify your chosen "I AM" essence.
- **Mindful Anchoring:** In the daily rush, it's easy to fall into reactive patterns. When challenges come up or emotions surge, anchor yourself with "I AM" awareness. Ask, "Which 'I AM' will guide my response?" Consciously choose the "I AM" essence that will lead the way.
- **Nature Walks with "I AM":** Head outdoors with a chosen "I AM" affirmation. As you walk, observe the environment through the lens of that affirmation. If your affirmation is "I AM abundant," notice the abundance in the leaves, the sounds, and sensations around you.
- **"I AM" Movement:** Embrace a movement or dance that channels your chosen "I AM." For "I AM freedom," for example, you might dance wildly and freely. For "I AM grounded," maybe a slow, deliberate tai chi or yoga sequence.
- **"I AM" Artistry:** Whether you paint, craft, sculpt, or doodle, create a piece of art that represents an "I AM" affirmation. It could be abstract or literal, but the act of creation will solidify your connection to your chosen identity.

THE ABDULLAH PARADOX: BELIEVING IS SEEING

What do you believe?

We've all heard the saying, "Seeing is believing." It makes sense that we need to see something with our own eyes to believe it. But what if you believed instead that "Believing is seeing"? In other words, we will see whatever we believe. This is a huge shift from the idea that our beliefs come from the world around us.

"Believing is seeing" is simple and revolutionary. It's not about wishful thinking. Abdullah's teachings are grounded in a deep understanding of the nature of consciousness. This age-old spiritual and philosophical wisdom challenges what we think we know.

"Believing is seeing" goes way back, long before Abdullah. Many ancient spiritual teachings and practices from different parts of the world have shared this concept.

In Hindu philosophy, there's a saying, "As is the individual, so is the universe." What we experience outside of us mirrors what's going on inside. There's a similar idea in Hermetic teachings: "As above, so below," or "As the inner, so the outer." What happens in the larger universe is reflected in our personal experiences and vice versa. The Bible's book of Mark says, "Whatever you ask for in prayer, believe that you have received it, and it will be yours" (NIV). The Yoruba religion believes in a connection between the spiritual realm (Orun) and the physical realm (Aye). Ancestors and deities or spirits, known as orishas, bridge the gap between these two realms. Through rituals, offerings, and prayers, practitioners align themselves with the energies of the orishas and manifest their desires in the physical world. The concept of "Nommo" in the Dogon people of Mali represents a primordial force that brought the universe into being through the power of the word. By invoking words and rituals, the Dogon believe they can shape reality. In the Waaqeffannaa belief system of the Oromo people in Ethiopia, rituals and prayers to Waaq, the one God, and ancestors actively shape the community's well-being and prosperity, emphasizing the idea that belief molds reality.

Exercises for Applying the Abdullah Paradox

- **Create a Belief Board:** Instead of a traditional vision board, create a belief board. For each goal or desire, write a corresponding belief. For example, if you want to travel more, write the belief "I AM an explorer." This reinforces your belief in the things you want to manifest.
- **Belief Enactment:** Live a day in your life as if your belief has already manifested. If you want to manifest being a successful author, spend a day in that role—write, choose your ideal publishers, or set up a profile for your work. Act as if it's already true.

- **Environment Design:** Design your surroundings to reflect your beliefs. If you believe you're wealthy, create an abundant environment—decorate your space with richness, elevate your workspace, and dress in a way that makes you feel prosperous.
- **Mindfulness Practices:** Develop mindfulness through practices like deep breathing or focused attention on your senses. This helps you stay present and anchored in your new belief, especially when external circumstances challenge it.

Exercises for Dealing with Your Own Skepticism and Doubt

- **Journaling:** Whenever doubt creeps in, write down your feelings. Explore the root of your skepticism and how you can address it. Writing can help you process your feelings and reaffirm your new beliefs.
- **Feedback Loop:** Find a trusted friend or mentor who supports your manifesting. Share your doubts and listen to their perspective. This can provide insights and help you stay grounded in your beliefs.
- **Reflect on Timing:** Your manifestation may not happen overnight. Believing is a process, and even if you don't see immediate results, your belief is still shaping your reality.

- **Cultivate Curiosity:** Instead of being defensive when faced with skepticism, become curious. Ask questions and seek to understand other perspectives without necessarily adopting them. "Believing is seeing" has the power to transform every aspect of your life and ripple out to affect the wider world. All it takes is a belief in the possibilities. Stay focused on your belief no matter what external circumstances show you.

WHAT DO YOU WANT?

Do you really want to go?

— ABDULLAH[2]

What do you want?

Decide. For every area of your life. Health, love, wealth, leisure, relationships, career, and purpose. I'm not talking about your safe dreams.

What do you really want? The scary, secret private dreams you dare not speak out loud.

What if I told you it is already done? From the moment you desire it, it is done.

But the first step to manifesting on purpose is to decide.

Every desire in your heart—from the small and seemingly irrelevant to the big, life-changing stuff—carries a unique cosmic vibration. Your desires form an integral part of life's grand design. They come from infinite intelligence and your soul's wisdom. Your desires summon you, enticing you to embrace a juicy life of purpose, richness, and joy.

Desire is a Divine gift and an invitation to Higher Consciousness. When we feel a strong desire for something, it is a sign that we are ready for a new level of experience and consciousness. Acknowledge your desires and follow their guidance to open yourself up to new opportunities, insights, and a greater sense of purpose.

Now, I know what you're thinking. I can manifest a designer bag or sexy new spouse? Yup. All of it. But that's just the tip of the iceberg. Yes, the readers that Abdullah and I called here want the dream houses, loving relationships, and cute clothes. But you also want the scholarships in your name, nonprofit givebacks, loving activism, and shifts in your family's generational calling.

The Divine energy that pulses through us all talks to us through nudges, hints, and signs. Every sign is like a small push, directing us toward experiences and achievements that match who we really are at our core. These synchronicities might seem like random coincidences, but they're really aligned plans to help us to create our future.

Your desires are expressions of the creativity inherent in our world. This highest power, be it the Universe, God, Source, or any other name that resonates with your understanding, within you and me, communicates its intentions through the language of desire.

By being open to this process of creating together, you make room for endless possibilities.

Connecting with your desires is lighting a spark. The moment you take on your real role as a creator this spark begins actively shaping your life.

Each desire, which comes from the deep wisdom of your soul, carries a unique energetic mark, like a special signature of your life. This mark represents your unique purpose in the big picture. When you line yourself up with the desires inspired by your soul, it's a compass to your true north. You naturally create opportunities and experiences that are good for you and others.

Your desires lead you to fulfill your soul's mission. Manifesting your desires allows you to leave a lasting impact, like a permanent record of your journey, what you learned, and how you've grown.

Your desires are important promises that the Divine energy within is ready and eager to make come true. Stop trying to control everything. Trust that everything is happening just as it should and for your benefit. This act of giving in (surrender) assumes complete faith and trust.

A student once asked Neville, "What is your technique of prayer?"

He answered:

> It starts with desire, for desire is the mainspring of action. You must know and define your objective, then condense it into a sensation which implies fulfillment. When your desire is clearly defined, immobilize your physical body and experience, in your imagination, the action which implies its fulfillment. Repeat this act over and over again until it has the vividness and feeling of reality.
>
> Or, condense your desire into a single phrase that implies fulfillment such as, "Thank you, Father," "Isn't it wonderful," or "It is finished." Repeat that condensed phrase or action in your imagination over and over again. Then either awaken from that state, or slip off into the deep. It does not matter, for the act is done when you completely accept it as being finished in that sleepy, drowsy state.[3]

Thankfulness opens a floodgate of blessings and invites a stream of goodness and prosperity. This strengthens your connection and fuels your deepest desires being born. Get clear about what you want, then use your imagination to feel and experience it as if it's already happened.

At first, I was thrown off when I read Neville's teaching "creation is finished." Then I realized that he meant that whenever you desire something, it already exists in a timeless spiritual realm. As Neville eloquently put it, "Because creation is finished, what you desire already exists. It is excluded from view because you can see only the contents of your own consciousness. It is the function of an assumption to call back the excluded view and restore full vision. It is not the world but your assumptions that change. An assumption brings the invisible into sight. It is nothing more nor less than seeing with the eye of God."[4] His teaching of 'creation is finished' is now what quantum manifestors refer to as multiple timelines.

Every single one of your desires exists in the fourth-dimensional world, ready to be occupied. This fourth-dimensional world, a realm beyond the constraints of time and space, holds your dreams, waiting for you to step into them. Your role as a conscious creator is to recognize that your desires are not distant dreams but existing realities within this higher dimension. By nurturing your desires with unwavering faith, and assuming the feeling of their fulfillment, you bridge the gap between the spiritual reality where "creation is finished" and our physical world. Desire propels you toward manifesting your deepest aspirations.

Exercise: Delving Deeper into Your Desires

Purpose: To uncover your desires. As you dare to claim your true desires, you free more of your authentic self.

1. What do you want? What desires are emerging for you? Are they based on material needs, personal growth, relationships, personal and spiritual evolution, or a combo of these? Write them down in your journal without judgment.
2. What emotions do your desires awaken in you? Do they turn you on, or evoke feelings of excitement, love, joy, or peace? Or do they stir feelings of anxiety, fear, or doubt?
3. How do your desires align with your purpose? Can you see a clear connection? If not, this is a great invitation to explore and learn your purpose.
4. What actions are you inspired to take, if any?
5. How will fulfilling these desires serve you and others?
6. What beliefs do you have about your desires? Do you believe they are possible to achieve? If you have secret doubts or pessimistic beliefs, they can be manifestation blocks. Identifying blocked beliefs is the first step to transforming them.
7. How can you cultivate gratitude for your desires? Gratitude accelerates manifestation.

WHAT IS CONSCIOUS MANIFESTING?

Conscious manifesting is a hidden superpower within each of us, waiting to be harnessed. It's the art of creating and shaping your life according to your dreams and desires, transforming imaginary possibilities into reality.

The truth is that you already are doing this. Yes, you are always manifesting, even when you are not aware of it. Every thought, belief, and emotion we hold sends signals and creates experiences and opportunities.

At the heart of manifesting is the concept of conscious creation. Conscious manifesting is the art of manifesting on purpose.

The modern social media manifesting movement will argue about whether your desires come because you are attracting them, jumping timelines, collaborating with the Divine, quantum shifting, or consciously creating new outcomes. Perhaps it's all of the above. What does it matter as long as you get the outcome you want.

Conscious manifesting involves deliberate and purposeful intention, aligning your thoughts and emotions with your desires. It's like crafting a blueprint for your dreams and then building them into reality, one imaginative thought at a time.

As I said before, manifesting is not new. It is universal law. That means that like gravity, it just is and it always was. Wisdom passed down through generations spoke of the interconnectedness between our inner worlds and the outer world. In ancient civilizations, sages and philosophers recognized the influence of thoughts and beliefs. Classical texts, like the Bible and other religious scriptures, contain teachings on manifesting, emphasizing the importance of faith, intention, and alignment with Divine will. Oral literature throughout many countries and cultures in Africa and Asia shared teachings like those of Abdullah.

In the late 19th and early 20th centuries, the New Thought movement in North America emerged as a powerful force for personal development and spiritual growth. Influential figures delved into mental healing and mind power, laying the groundwork for manifesting principles that still resonate.

In 2006, a groundbreaking movie named *The Secret* captivated audiences worldwide. I remember telling all of my friends, "Hey, you MUST see this movie. It changes everything!" This documentary by Rhonda Byrne, publicized by Oprah Winfrey, brought the concept of manifesting into mainstream consciousness. *The Secret* introduced the Law of Attraction—the idea that like attracts like, and that by aligning our thoughts with our desires, we can attract positive outcomes into our lives.

Oprah was instrumental in bringing the Law of Attraction into mainstream awareness. Through her talk show and media platforms, she introduced millions to books and key figures in the self-help community. Her endorsement shifted manifesting from a niche topic to dinner conversation.

After *The Secret*, "Abraham Hicks," channeled by Esther Hicks, became a major force in the Law of Attraction community. They introduced nuanced concepts like "vibrational alignment," enriching the movement.

Countless people explored the potential of their thoughts and intentions. Folks learned that they had more power than they thought over themselves and their lives. This is a wonderful thing! I was already trying many of these practices. The mainstreaming of it allowed me to come out of the closet as a "Secret Manifestor."

Purposeful manifesting has evolved into an essential aspect of conscious living. Abdullah's impact remains, as teachings from Abdullah's students, including Neville and Dr. Joseph Murphy, continue to shape modern manifesting. Their insights into the mind and its creative potential have made a long-standing mark.

Conscious manifesting is not really mysterious or esoteric. It is a practical and empowering, real approach to shaping your reality deliberately. At its core, conscious manifesting involves being aware of the creative power of your thoughts, beliefs, and emotions and intentionally aligning them with your desired outcomes.

In the realm of manifesting, there are two distinct approaches: conscious and unconscious manifestation. Unconscious manifestation occurs when we are not fully aware of the thoughts and beliefs driving our experiences. Conscious manifestation is actively engaging with our thoughts and emotions.

Setting clear intentions is like using GPS. When you identify your true desires, you establish a direction for your manifesting. Conscious manifesting encourages us to be honest with ourselves and recognize what brings us joy.

You have the power to shape your reality. Embrace this truth with unwavering belief and gratitude.

Critics argue that an overemphasis on "positive thinking" can promote toxic positivity and spiritual bypassing, sidelining real issues like trauma, systemic inequality, or mental health struggles. Make sure that your pursuit of manifesting complements, rather than replaces, your emotional and psychological healing.

THE POWER OF IMAGINATION

Now clothe yourself with Barbados.
Put it on as you would another garment,
just as you would another garment, so that you
would smell the tropics and you would
see were you in Barbados.

— *Abdullah*

Close your eyes and imagine yourself living your desired reality. The alchemical process that turns thoughts into reality is within the realm of your imagination. Feel the warm embrace of love, smell the success, hear the applause, taste the moment, and feel the fulfillment.

At the very core of our human consciousness is the gift of imagination.

Neville said, "If the word God, in any way, conjures within you something that is other than your own wonderful human imagination, you've got the wrong God." True understanding of God is not as something separate or external but as an intrinsic and indwelling aspect of our own consciousness and creative abilities. Neville explains, "Your own wonderful human imagination is the actual creative power of God within you."

Your imagination creates your reality. The essence of your imagination is your God consciousness within.

This may sound "out there" now, but as you embrace the power of your imagination, you'll witness miracles unfold. Your thoughts, dreams, and intentions shape the reality you experience. Yes, imagination creates reality.

Abdullah said, "All heaven obeys the little child. All earth is compelled to manifest that which the heavens obey, and they obey only the voice of the little child. You must always forever think of the Christos as the little child." Abdullah's teachings emphasize that Christ consciousness is intimately connected with our imaginative and creative manifesting abilities, like the limitless imagination of a child. Recognizing and aligning with this innate creative power within influences both the spiritual and material dimensions of reality. In this context, "the little child" signifies humanity, highlighting that we possess the divine gift of imagination and creative manifestation, like to the boundless imagination of a little child.

As kids, imagination was our gateway to adventure and possibility. We could be anything we wanted and explore places far beyond the limits of our physical world. Growing up in a Caribbean family in New York City, I loved to daydream. My daydreams and playtime took the form of writing stories, rapping, playing with dolls, jumping double Dutch, roller-skating and drawing, just for starters!

My imagination, along with the vision boards it helped me create on my bright yellow bedroom walls, helped me escape from the drama of life around me. Imagining let me create my own worlds where I could explore my thoughts and feelings, and experience the beauty and ugliness of childhood.

In my imagination I could create anything and be anyone. Now, as an adult, I've realized that imagination is a force that shapes reality. It's much more than child's play or the domain of quirky artists (speaking as a quirky artist), as society tries to have us believe. Imagining is an ability that each one of us has, and it affects your life.

We have all experienced how imagination can make you feel anxious, worried, or excited about an event that hasn't happened. You might have created a worst-case scenario in your head and felt its physical effects: a pounding heart, nervousness, or sweaty palms. On the other hand, when you visualize—or imagine—a positive outcome, you most likely feel relaxed, confident, or happy. This is your imagination at work.

Now, imagine using this power to shape your life intentionally. Everything ever invented or humanly created started in someone's imagination. Let's get more specific.

What if I told you your imagination is the God-force?

That's the essence of Abdullah's teachings—and those of his star pupil, Neville.

Neville taught that our beliefs and feelings, shaped by our imagination, reflect in our external circumstances. If you change your inner world, your external reality will follow suit. He emphasized that we are the creators of our own reality and that by using our imagination and feeling our wish fulfilled, we can attract and manifest our desires.

Abdullah introduced Neville to the esoteric metaphysical power of using imagination for transformation.

Let's go back to move forward . . . In 1933, as the bitter winds of the Great Depression swept the country, my beloved New York City was a place of struggle. The Great Depression was a global economic crisis that spanned from 1929 to 1939. Soup kitchens, bread lines, unemployment, and misery mixed with despair. Jobs were hella scarce, and the once-thriving spirit of the Big Apple was a distant memory.

Abdullah lived in a beautiful residence on West 72nd Street, previously owned by the father of the country's treasurer. At a time when hope was in short supply, Abdullah personified resilience.

Neville, a renowned dancer, found himself in a city where Broadway shows were no longer a luxury people could afford. But in the middle of the gloom he found a glimmer of hope as he cleaned Abdullah's home in exchange for a metaphysical apprenticeship.

Neville's family came from Barbados for a visit, and as soon as they left and the October chill settled in, Neville felt homesick. He hadn't been back to Barbados in 12 years. He confessed to Abdullah that he was longing to spend Christmas at home with his family. The only problem? He was completely broke.

Abdullah's determined response surprised Neville: "You are in Barbados."[5]

Neville said, "I am in Barbados?"

He said, "Yes. You are now in Barbados. And so . . . you see Barbados, and you see America from Barbados, and you can smell the tropical land of Barbados, see only the little homes of Barbados, and that's all you do. You just simply sleep this night in Barbados."

This is the power of your imagination.

"If you want to go, Neville, you have gone." Abdullah insisted.

"What do you mean, I have gone, Abdullah?"

"Do you really want to go?" he asked.

"Yes," Neville answered.

Abdullah replied with the magic formula for manifestation: "As you walk through this door now you are not walking on 72nd Street, you are walking on palm-lined streets, coconut-lined streets. This is Barbados. Do not ask me how you are going to go. You are in Barbados. You do not say 'how' when you 'are there.' You are there. Now you walk as though you were there."[6]

Abdullah instructed Neville to live as if he were already there, to imagine the smell of the tropics, enjoy the charm of the island homes, see himself in his mother's house.

Neville said, "Well, I thought him insane, really . . . I mean, at the moment, it seemed so . . . stupid."

Even though he was thoroughly confused by Abdullah's advice, Neville followed it. He immersed himself in his imagination, especially every night before falling asleep. He saw himself walking through his family home, feeling the Caribbean breeze, hearing the waves, and basking in the joy of his loved ones.

Weeks passed, and reality still hadn't caught up to Neville's imaginings. He tried to discuss his frustrations over the lack of results with Abdullah. But Abdullah, unwavering in his belief, slammed the door in his face, stating that there was no need to discuss a trip that had already happened. Abdullah believed for Neville when he was unable to do so.

December came, and despite his imaginal efforts, Neville was still in New York, his faith wavering. But Abdullah still stood firm, confident that once you commit fully to a belief that something will happen, the "how" becomes irrelevant. In his eyes, Neville was already in Barbados.

And then, like a miracle, a letter arrived. Neville's brother invited him to spend Christmas in Barbados and sent him a ticket. Although he could only afford third class, Neville was overjoyed. He rushed to tell Abdullah, expecting him to be surprised. But Abdullah simply said, "Who told you that you are going to Barbados? And who told you that you went to Barbados third class? You went to Barbados, and you went first class."

Abdullah was already speaking of the trip in past tense. Soon, Neville made the voyage to Barbados, just as he imagined. He was able to travel first class through a mysterious last-minute cancellation and spent three blissful months at home.

Abdullah, of course, was not surprised.[7]

Now, it's your turn. Completely immerse yourself in the feeling that your dream is already realized. Nurture that feeling and protect it until it becomes your physical reality.

It's not about how you'll achieve it. The magic key is to live as if your dream has already come true. When you have planted the seed of your dream, let it grow without interference.

Neville's trip home to Barbados is a powerful example of how divine imagination can transform your life. I have used this exact formula to manifest "impossible" things. Abdullah's unshakeable faith in Neville's dream shows that imagining isn't just about visualizing an end goal. It's about living every detail of your desired reality until it's part of who you are. You become someone different. Neville became someone who had already reunited with his family in first class, and then it happened afterward in the physical. Embracing this power needs persistent faith and total alignment with what you desire.

Tap into your divine imagination. This is the force that creates your desires. Life may throw challenges your way, but you can navigate any obstacle. Your goals are pushing you toward your purpose.

When your dreams seem out of reach, remind yourself of Abdullah's unwavering faith and the power of your divine imagination. Whether it's a dream home, a romance, or an empowerment retreat, if you can see it, feel it, imagine and believe it, you're already there.

PART II:

THE LAW OF LIFE

I have heard it before with the hearing of my ear, but now my eye seeth it.

— Abdullah

My Dear Esteemed Seeker,

I bring you ancient wisdom of the Law of Life, revealing the transformative power within you. This law is simple but requires unwavering steadfast faith. Your imagination is your gateway to making your desires manifest. Assume the feeling of your desires fulfilled and you shall create your reality.

Hold fast to your belief and assumption, and watch as the world around you mirrors the beauty and splendor of your imagination.

The Law of Life is your birthright.

With the deepest respect and blessings,

Your Teacher

When we hear the words "the Law" in the world of manifesting, most of us jump straight to the "Law of Attraction," but there's so much more to manifesting than that. There's an entire universe of spiritual laws.

We've been delving into the lessons of Abdullah's student Neville. But what about Dr. Joseph Murphy? He taught the "Law of Belief." Even though Neville and Murphy used different names for the Law, their teachings boil down to the same basic idea: our beliefs and assumptions create our lives.

Think about it like this: Neville's Law of Assumption is all about assuming your dream life is already here. By thinking, feeling, and behaving as if your desires are already a reality, you're sending a strong message to your "I AM" Consciousness. You're saying, "I'm ready for this!"

Dr. Murphy's Law of Belief is like a powerful engine for creation. When you deeply believe in your dreams, you're shaping them into reality. Your belief acts like a creative force, bringing everything you want into existence in your life.

Together, to represent Abdullah's key teachings, I call them the "Law of Life" or "the Law."

In this chapter, we're going to the heart of the Law. This isn't just some abstract idea. It's a real, living force that's present in every moment. When we align with the Law, we tap into our power to make our world as we desire it to be. We're no longer just going through the motions. You are consciously creating your reality with purpose and love.

So, let's dive in and explore the Law together!

LAW OF ATTRACTION

The Law of Attraction taught us that our dreams attract corresponding experiences into our lives. So, naturally, we, the believers got busy creating visual representations of our desires called vision boards and trying to go high vibe and "think positive" to manifest our stuff.

The Law of Attraction worked for many, but for many others there was a missing link.

So, let's go back to the source material. Rhonda Byrne, creator of *The Secret*, was influenced directly by Neville Goddard. Neville was taught by Abdullah.

Many found themselves frustrated with their vision boards, affirmations, and failed attempts at positive thinking. The charges of toxic positivity and spiritual bypassing left folks feeling disillusioned and yelling "Cancel! Cancel!" if they couldn't stay high vibe. I heard it again and again, "Abiola, the Law of Attraction didn't work for me." Folks wondered why their dreams weren't materializing despite trying to align with their desires. The disgruntled and frustrated labeled the whole thing a crock of crap.

What was missing? Well, the first thing is that there are many universal laws. The Law of Attraction is just one of them.

Introducing the Law of Life

As students of Abdullah, I want to introduce you to a powerful, unified concept that will serve as your guiding star: the Law of Life, or simply the Law. Whatever you call it, this potent universal law is the key to your manifestation journey. The Law of Life combines the wisdom of two time-tested principles—the Law of Assumption and the Law of Belief—into one dynamic law that holds the key to manifesting your dream life. While the Law of Assumption and the Law of Belief are both powerful in their own right, they are intrinsically intertwined, working together to shape our realities. The Law of Belief lays the foundation, while the Law of Assumption drives us to action.

The Law of Life is based on two essential pillars:

Believe It: The first step is to deeply believe in your dreams. These aren't just passing thoughts or whimsical wishes. These are your deepest desires, the ones that resonate with your heart and soul. Your beliefs are the bedrock of your reality, the fertile soil for your desires.

Assume It: Building on your beliefs, start assuming that your desires are already a reality. Live, act, and make decisions as if your dreams have already come true. This goes beyond pretending or denying your current circumstances. It's about aligning your actions with your beliefs and creating a synergy that propels you toward your dreams.

These are two sides of the same coin and are both essential in the manifestation process. Combining these two pillars, the Law of Life becomes your personal co-creation tool.

The Law of Life is our way of coming full circle to the teachings of our great spiritual mentor Abdullah. We are embracing the fullness of Abdullah's teachings by recognizing them as a unified concept. However, I have to point out that even though we are combining these principles, these two laws still exist separately and hold their individual significance. If you find comfort and resonance in the language of the Law of Assumption or the Law of Belief, continue to use those terms. They remain valid and powerful concepts in their own right.

Abdullah's teachings were about more than just words. He encouraged his students and us to step into our power, to believe in the possibility of our desires, and to live as if these desires already existed.

The Law of Life is your key to unlocking a world of infinite possibilities. Trust in its power, follow its principles, and prepare to experience a life beyond your expectations.

The Missing Link

The Law of Attraction teaches you to visualize your dreams and maintain a positive mindset, acting like a magnet to draw good things your way. While helpful, this is just the starting point. The Law of Life goes further. It insists that you deeply believe and assume that your dreams are already a reality. You act, feel, and make decisions as if your desires have already manifested. This is what Neville called "assuming the feeling of the wish fulfilled."

Many people who find the Law of Attraction lacking often miss out on this crucial internal shift. They focus only on attracting external desires and overlook the need to internally assume the state of those desires being fulfilled. This assumption is vital because it aligns your energy frequency with your dreams, signaling that you already have what you want.

Here's the key: By embracing the Law of Life, you actively participate in shaping the reality you desire. This approach empowers you to align your thoughts, emotions, and actions with the state of already fulfilling your dreams. By doing so, you're not just attracting experiences toward you. You are consciously *creating* your manifestations.

So, if you tried the Law of Attraction and it hasn't worked out, don't lose hope! This change in perspective can help your dreams come true in ways you might never have imagined.

Life is always working in your favor.

The Power of Belief

Dr. Murphy's philosophy revolves around the potential hidden in our subconscious minds. He taught the Law of Belief as the way to unlock this untapped power. He put it this way: "What you believe with feeling, conviction, and faith is what will be manifested in your life."

Your beliefs create your destiny. The more you understand this, the more empowered you become to manifest.

Embracing the role of a conscious creator empowers us to take charge of our beliefs and, as a result, our reality. Every day, we encounter all kinds of situations. Our beliefs assign meaning and significance to them. When we hold positive beliefs about ourselves, others, and the world, our experiences tend to be more uplifting and fulfilling. Negative, blocked, or limiting beliefs can cloud your vision and stop you from recognizing opportunities and possibilities.

Your beliefs determine the story of your life. Being aware of the beliefs that drive your thoughts and actions changes the narrative you tell yourself.

Beliefs, Thoughts, and Emotions

Beliefs, thoughts, and emotions influence each other in a continuous cycle. Your beliefs shape your thoughts, and your thoughts affect your emotions.

When you hold positive beliefs about yourself and your potential, your thoughts naturally focus on opportunities and achievement, leading to emotions like joy, hope, and love. Blocked beliefs increase doubt and fear in your thoughts, which then manifest as undesired emotions like anxiety and despair. This can become a vicious cycle that reinforces blocked beliefs.

You have the power to break this cycle by consciously choosing positive thoughts and cultivating good feelings. This reshapes and improves your beliefs, which creates a ripple effect that transforms your reality.

Beliefs act like filters, coloring our perception of the world. They give meaning to our experiences and play a significant role in shaping how we interpret events. If you believe in your abilities and see the world as full of opportunities, you'll still feel hopeful when faced with challenges. If you have blocked beliefs, you might feel anxious and uncertain even in the face of positive developments.

The exciting part is that you can change these beliefs by becoming aware of them and making a conscious choice to see the world differently. Focus on empowering thoughts to cultivate a more positive outlook and open up a world of new possibilities.

Even though it may seem like it, our beliefs are never fixed. Beliefs are flexible and malleable. Yes, some beliefs feel harder to shift than others, but beliefs can be transformed. We have the power to choose and modify our beliefs to align them with our desires and objectives.

The more we think certain thoughts or experience specific situations, the stronger the neural pathways become, making beliefs more resistant to change. Repetition helps solidify beliefs. By carefully choosing our thoughts and using tools like affirmations and visualization, we create new neural networks that support our growth and well-being.

The practices in this book and tools like hypnosis, intention, and visualizing can help you rewire your brain and reshape your beliefs. By aligning your thoughts and emotions with your desires, you can manifest the reality you want.

So, What Are Blocked Beliefs?

If you've ever found yourself holding back, self-sabotaging, or feeling like your actions don't align with your intentions, you've come face-to-face with your own success blocks or blocked beliefs.

Blocked beliefs can also be called limiting beliefs, blocked thought patterns, negative assumptions, subconscious blocks, mental roadblocks, self-defeating thoughts, or destructive mindsets.

Here are some common blocked beliefs that might sound familiar:

- **I am not enough.** This belief convinces you that you don't deserve happiness, success, or love, leading to self-esteem issues.
- **I'm not ready yet.** This belief convinces you that you'll only be good enough once certain conditions are met, like losing weight, making more money, or finding an ideal relationship.

It can tie your self-worth to external circumstances.

- **It's too late.** This belief convinces you that you missed your chance, holding you back from taking risks and exploring new opportunities.
- **Just my luck.** Whether it's missing out on opportunities or expecting the worst in every situation, this belief reinforces the victim story that you have no control over your circumstances.

The influence of blocked beliefs goes far beyond just thoughts. They permeate every aspect of our lives, influencing our behavior, decisions, and relationships. Like a self-fulfilling prophecy, these beliefs become a filter we use to see the world. They alter our perceptions.

The path to breaking free from blocked beliefs begins with awareness and self-compassion. Take a moment to reflect on your thoughts and identify any recurring patterns of negativity or self-doubt. Recognize that it's entirely normal to have limiting beliefs; we all carry them to some extent. The key is to acknowledge their presence without judgment.

Once you've identified these beliefs, challenge them. Ask yourself if they are based on concrete evidence or stories that no longer serve you. Unravel the thoughts and emotions tied to these beliefs. They don't define your worth or potential.

Aligned Empowering Beliefs

The other side of the coin to blocked beliefs is empowering beliefs. Empowering beliefs uplift your spirit, spark your imagination, and fuel your passion. Empowering beliefs cheer you on and remind you that you are capable, deserving, and destined for greatness. Embrace these beliefs, and you'll find the courage to step outside your comfort zone and manifest your dreams.

Here are some examples of empowering beliefs:

- **I deserve success and abundance.** Remind yourself that you are worthy of all the goodness life has to offer. Embrace the prosperity that surrounds you, knowing that success is your birthright.
- **Every challenge is an opportunity for growth.** Shift your perspective and see challenges as stepping stones. Embrace the lessons they offer, and transform setbacks into learning experiences.
- **I have the wisdom to make the right choices.** Trust in your inner wisdom and the ability to make decisions that serve your highest good. Embrace your intuition.
- **I am capable of achieving my goals.** Embrace your inner strength and believe in your abilities. You have the power to turn dreams into reality.

What if you had unwavering faith in your worthiness and potential? Picture yourself believing that life is on your side, aligning orchestrating circumstances to support your dreams. Imagine embracing the belief that abundance and success are meant for you, inviting prosperity into every part of your life.

Beliefs are not passive. They actively influence our thoughts and actions. As conscious co-creators, we choose the beliefs that shape our world. When we believe in our dreams and embrace empowering beliefs, our assumptions naturally align with what we envision.

Through your beliefs, you are the conscious creator of your life's masterpiece. The magic lies within you!

Exercise: Upgrade Your Mind with Belief-Shifting

Purpose: To help you dig deeper into your subconscious mind and replace blocked beliefs with positive, empowering ones.

What to do:

1. **Identify your focus areas.** Decide which areas of your life you want to focus on. Some key areas could include health, romance, family, career, finance, and personal growth. Write each area as a heading on a new page in your journal.
2. **List your beliefs.** Under each heading, list all of your current beliefs in that specific area. Be as real and thorough as possible. Write down everything that comes to mind, even if it seems irrelevant. For example, under "Career," you might list beliefs like "I must work hard to succeed," or "I'm not good with people."
3. **Examine your beliefs.** Once you make your lists, review each belief and ask yourself, "Does this belief serve me (empowering belief) or hold me back (blocked belief)?" If the belief contributes to your growth and happiness, it's serving you. If the belief creates fear or doubt, it's limiting you.
4. **Challenge blocked beliefs.** Now, focus on the beliefs holding you back. For each one, ask yourself, "Why do I have this belief? Is it based

on my own experiences, or is it from somewhere else? Is there evidence that contradicts this belief?" Be curious and open-minded as you investigate each belief.

5. **Replace blocked beliefs.** For every limiting belief, come up with a positive, empowering belief to replace it. Write this new belief down next to the old one. For example, if your blocked belief is "I'm not good at speaking," you might replace it with "I have lots to say and I can become a better speaker with practice."

6. **Affirm your new beliefs.** Reinforce your new beliefs daily. Say them out loud every morning, write them on sticky notes, and place them where you'll see them throughout the day. Incorporate them into your daily meditation or visualization practice. The goal is to instill these new beliefs in your subconscious mind and replace your old ones.

THE POWER OF ASSUMPTION

If you want to go, you have gone. You are there.
Now walk as though you were there.

— *Abdullah*

We shifted major energy with the Law of Belief. Let's dive into the other key part of the Law of Life: the Law of Assumption. The Law of Assumption invites us to assume that our desires are already fulfilled. It asks us to embody the feeling and belief that what we seek is already a part of our reality. Instead of longing for something in the future, we step into the energetic state of already having received it right now. Then it must come to you. That is law.

Imagine this: You want to manifest your dream job. Instead of obsessing over the lack of it, you assume the feeling of success, abundance, and fulfillment that comes with already having your dream career. You walk, talk, and act as if it's already yours. This shift in assumption changes your energetic vibration, aligning you with the frequency of your desires.

Let's get specific.

Here are a few examples of the Law of Assumption in action from my Womanifesting community:

- **Boldness Boost:** Lisette struggled with confidence. She assumed the state of a secure person. She carried herself with confident postures. She made bold decisions she had put on the back burner. She felt the excitement of trusting herself. It sounds simple, but she didn't even notice how much her self-confidence increased until everyone started asking what she was doing differently.
- **Job Promotion:** Mariah was secretly aiming for a work promotion. She stopped waiting and hoping. She embodied the thoughts (mindset) and behaviors of the new position. She felt the satisfaction of already having the role, and started to be treated with the respect of her desired position. And just like that, after seven weeks her dream promotion was offered. She ended up not taking it because an even better job seemingly came out of nowhere.
- **Finding Love:** Ayana wanted a loving, committed partner. As an experiment she released the desperation and started to live as if she were already in a beautiful, fulfilling relationship. She rearranged her home so her love-to-be would be comfy there. She moved and dressed like someone in love. She felt the security and happiness love brings. She noticed a shift in how the people she knew and total strangers responded to her. In a little over four months she attracted the relationship she was embodying.
- **Wealth Manifestation:** Sala dreamed of being financially independent. She started to live as if she was already wealthy. She felt the freedom

and security that prosperity brings. She made decisions, giving and receiving the way a wealthy person would. Sala started creating and attracting new opportunities that increased her prosperity.

- **Successful Business:** Nicole launched a new Spiritpreneur business. She decided to live as if the business was already thriving. She set her rates with the confidence of a successful entrepreneur. Her next course launch doubled her business with soulmate clients.
- **Overcoming Fear:** Amber had a fear of flying but dreamed of traveling. She imagined the thrill and freedom of traveling to tropical places. She joined a fun, sexy travel club. Her fear diminished. The money came from "nowhere" and she attended my last international retreat.

In each of these situations, it was crucial for them to wholeheartedly assume their desired state—to feel it, live it, and know it as their current reality. Most of them supplemented their assumptions with the processes at the back of this book, but some of them were able to move forward with assumption alone.

A Guide to Unlocking the Power of the Law of Assumption

So how can you leverage the Law of Assumption to manifest your desires and aspirations?

- **Identify and define your desire.** As we discussed in "The Foundation," you have to know what your wish is before you can assume the feeling of your wish fulfilled. Spend time defining your desire. Make it clear, concise, and compelling. What is it that you want? Focus on the end result, not how you'll get there. Leave the "how" to the Divine.

- **Embrace the feeling of the wish fulfilled.** The Law of Assumption is not about intellectualizing your desire. It's about embodying the emotional and physical state of your wish fulfilled. You feel and live as if your desire is already a reality. How would you feel if your desire was already manifested? What would you feel? Joy, relief, freedom, peace, safety, sexiness, thankfulness, giddiness, love, excitement, or satisfaction? Cultivate these feelings right now.
- **Incorporate your assumptions into daily life.** Once you identify the emotions associated with your wish fulfilled, start incorporating these feelings into your daily life. As you go about your day, continuously return to these emotions. Live as if your desired state is your current reality. Make decisions from this state. Ask yourself: "As someone who has already achieved this, how would I act? What choices would I make?" By acting from your desired state, you strengthen your assumption and signal that this is your reality.
- **Practice persistence and consistency.** Consistency is key in the application of the Law of Assumption. Persist in your assumption and return to your desired state until it becomes a natural part of your consciousness.
- **Face contradictory beliefs.** Sometimes, we carry deep-seated beliefs that contradict our conscious desires. These beliefs can block your manifestations. If you notice resistance or doubt creeping in as you try to embody your

desired state, identify these blocked beliefs and work on transforming them. You can use techniques like affirmations, meditation, therapy, or journaling to uncover and reframe these beliefs. When your subconscious mind is aligned with your conscious desires, the Law can work more effectively.

- **Surrender to the outcome.** Surrender is an integral aspect of conscious manifesting. Yes, it's essential to actively assume the state of your goal fulfilled, but it's equally important to let go and allow the Divine to orchestrate the details. Your role is to provide the emotional blueprint through your assumption. Trust in the process and allow.
- **Express gratitude.** Expressing gratitude for your desire as if it has already manifested amplifies the energy of your assumption. It sends a clear signal to Divine Consciousness that you recognize and appreciate the fulfillment of your desire. Make gratitude a part of your daily practice.
- **Keep growing and evolving.** The more you practice and apply it, the better you'll become at consciously creating your reality.

Why the Law of Life Sometimes Seems to Fail

The Law of Life (Law of Assumption + Law of Belief) is always at work. But sometimes we unknowingly block ourselves from its full potential.

Here's what could be going wrong for you:

- **You're not really believing in your goal.** You've got to do more than just hope or daydream. Live like your dream is already real. If you're not sure about it, that can slow you down. Believe and act like your goal is happening.

- **You're not sticking with it.** Using the Law of Life takes practice. If you live in your dream one day and forget about it the next, your subconscious mind might not get the message. Be consistent.
- **You're holding conflicting beliefs.** If your deeper beliefs disagree with your conscious goals, it can slow you down. For example, you might want to be rich but secretly think that money is bad. These hidden beliefs can block your progress.
- **You're not feeling it.** Manifesting isn't just about positive thinking. It's about genuinely feeling the emotions tied to your dream, like happiness and excitement. It also means addressing and transforming any negative emotions that may come up, like fear of success. Embrace the full spectrum of emotions to enhance your manifesting power.
- **You're impatient or doubtful.** The Law of Life takes time and trust. Sometimes we mess things up by being too eager or not believing in the process. Let go of the rush and trust that your dream will happen when it's supposed to.
- **You're making it too complicated.** Sometimes we think the Law needs to be hard. But it's not about doing a bunch of processes. The processes are just to support The Law. Decide what you want, believe it's real, feel it, and live it every day. Keep it simple.
- **You're trying too hard.** Sometimes we push too much to make the Law work. If you're feeling

stressed about it, relax and trust the process. Let your desires flow to you naturally.

- **You're talking or thinking negatively.** The Law responds to what we most often think and say. Speak as if your dream is already real. If you find yourself thinking negatively, gently switch to positive thoughts.

These are stumbling blocks, not dead ends. The Law of Life always works. It's about how you use it. By knowing these pitfalls, you can use the Law of Life to intentionally create the life you want–and deserve.

Your Law of Life Journal Questions

- What beliefs or assumptions have been holding me back, and how can I shift them to align with the life I desire?
- How can I tune in to my intuition, listen to my inner guidance, and take actions that align with the Law of Life?
- How can I embody the feelings and emotions associated with my dreams and desires, and what practices can help me maintain this emotional alignment with the Law of Life?
- Recall a moment in your life when you really wanted something but couldn't see any evidence that it was possible. How would your feelings and actions have been different if you had fully embraced the Law of Life?
- See one of your deepest desires as already fulfilled. Write a detailed description of a day in your life where you've achieved this dream. Notice your emotions, thoughts, and actions.

PART III:

THE 13 MANIFESTING SCROLLS OF ABDULLAH

Greetings, Esteemed Reader,

You now hold a repository of ancient manifesting principles distilled from my years of inquiry, introspection, and study. As you immerse yourself in these 13 Manifesting Scrolls, you are embarking upon a voyage of self-discovery and personal metamorphosis.

Each scroll extends to you an invitation to access the power of potential. Discover the keys to aligning your intentions with your most fervent desires, thereby creating a life of love, abundance, jubilation, and well-being. Steep yourself in each scroll to awaken an unwavering belief in the power of your creative imagination.

The world before you is yours to shape, and you are the artisan who crafts the episodes of your existence. Receive these teachings with an open heart and willing mind.

Welcome, dear reader, to a world where you are loved unconditionally by the Divine presence, and you are sovereign in your own life.

Assume your role as the deliberate architect of your existence.

Your Teacher

In the following pages, you will discover the 13 Manifesting Scrolls of Abdullah, a transformative compendium of spiritual laws, mysteries, decrees, affirmations, and actionable advice.

Each scroll contains a unique insight into the power of conscious creation. These scrolls are a road map, guiding you toward a life of intentional manifestation, where your dreams become reality.

Abdullah's scrolls are a testament to his life's work. His legacy has inspired millions to awaken their power and create the life they really want.

By practicing these principles consistently, you will begin to notice subtle shifts in your reality, as your desires begin to materialize and your life aligns with your highest aspirations.

Let these scrolls serve as a reminder that you are the creator of your destiny, and you hold the power to shape your life.

THE MYSTERY OF SELF-CONCEPT

You must start with the self. Find self,
don't be ashamed ever of the being you are.
Discover it and start the changing of that self.[1]

— Abdullah[1]

Let's take another trip back to between 1929 and 1939. Prejudice and racism were legal, overwhelmingly overt, and uberpresent. The Ku Klux Klan rained down terror and fear in a resurgence known as the Bloody '20s with lynchings, arson, and intimidation, holding marches even in the north from New Jersey to Washington, D.C. The artistic and intellectually vibrant Harlem Renaissance was waning due to the impact of the Great Depression. Harlem residents faced housing discrimination, overcrowding, and exploitative landlords. United Negro Improvement Association founder Marcus Garvey was deported back to Jamaica in 1927 for advocating for Black empowerment.

Public spaces, such as hotels, restaurants, and pools either explicitly excluded Black people or made it clear we were unwelcome. Just like today, Black residents in the North and South alike frequently experienced unjustified arrests, beatings, and other forms of abuse by law enforcement. Black workers were relegated to the lowest-paying menial jobs, if they could find work at all.

Josephine Baker moved to Paris in the 1920s to escape American racial discrimination and segregation. In the near future of 1938, Billie Holiday will break barriers as one of the first Black woman vocalists with a white orchestra, but will be prohibited from eating with the band or staying in the same hotels. Marian Anderson was a contralto who gained international acclaim in the 1930s but would have to wait until 1955 to become the first Black person to perform at the Metropolitan Opera in New York City.

During this time, a person of color wouldn't dare to go up to any ticket booth outside of a Black neighborhood to ask for a seat in the front section. We were only allowed in the balcony seats, if at all. Those were the rules.

But Abdullah didn't play by these rules.

Abdullah didn't just accept "that's the way it is." He didn't allow his white friends to purchase tickets for him. An opera aficionado, Abdullah would walk straight up to the ticket booth, not caring about the dangers and biases of the times. With an unwavering voice, he'd command, "I want two in the center. I don't want too far back. Not beyond the sixth row. Right in the center."

The response? "Yes, sir." Without missing a beat, he'd get two tickets to any show his heart desired.

Neville had his first experience with opera courtesy of Abdullah.

"You go on Good Friday in New York," Abdullah said. So they attended Wagner epic *Parsifal* together.

Abdullah's choice of *Parsifal* on Good Friday was a layered message. In the opera, Parsifal sets out to find the Holy Grail, a symbol of spiritual awakening and achieving desires. Good Friday is the day in Christian tradition associated with the crucifixion of Jesus Christ and His subsequent resurrection. Abdullah's message here is to embrace your inner journey and the capacity for rebirth, transform your consciousness, and embody the qualities needed for successful manifesting and spiritual growth.

Abdullah's audacity in walking up to the box office and demanding his rightful place in the orchestra section was revolutionary. He was a dark-skinned Black man and foreign-born in an era that denied people like him their due respect and dignity. Yet, there he was, challenging the status quo with the simple act of purchasing an opera ticket.

Abdullah's attitude of deservedness was rooted in his self-concept, which you may also call his identity. Abdullah held a firm belief in his self-worth. He was unshaken by societal norms and prejudices. He understood his worth as a human being, not defined by his race, but his inherent value. Abdullah's rock-solid self-concept empowered him to navigate spaces traditionally closed to people like him and engage in experiences he appreciated.

Abdullah's conviction in his own worthiness allowed him to act confidently and command respect where others might have felt insecure or fearful of racist repercussions. For me, Abdullah purchasing those tickets was more than just gaining access to a cultural event; it was a declaration of his personal power and a strong statement against expectations. The strength of his self-belief paved the way for his own empowerment and served as a beacon of inspiration for others, including Neville—and me.

To give some perspective on the power of Abdullah's self-concept, I remember walking along East 86th Street 10 minutes from the opera house in middle school. I felt simultaneously hypervisible and invisible in my Black skin. I felt insecure walking into stores, restaurants, and just being. This was the late '80s, obviously post-civil rights movement, but I had been conditioned and socialized by much in my environment to question my deservedness and worth, even as a child. Before Uber and Lyft, I always had my white friends flag taxis for me in New York. So the image of Abdullah refusing the safety of having his white friends purchase his ticket was a powerful one for me.

What Is Self-Concept?

Change your conception of yourself and you will automatically change the world in which you live. Do not try to change people; they are only messengers telling you who you are. Revalue yourself and they will confirm the change.

— Neville

Your self-concept is your self image, how you see the world, and how you see yourself in it. We can also consider this to be your identity. Your self-concept is made of the internal stories or maps we hold that guide our experiences and possibilities. This identity includes the deep-rooted beliefs and assumptions that influence how we see the world and what we believe is possible.

Your self-concept is the story you tell yourself about who you are, encompassing your personality traits, your abilities, your values, your role in the world, and even how much abundance and joy you believe you're entitled to.

When you use phrases like, "People like me/us," "I always or never," "That's how I am," or "Things like that always happen to me . . ." you are revealing your self-concept.

For example, my mother and aunts often use the phrase, "Poor people like us . . ." One day, I asked my mom about it and she wasn't even aware she does it. She inherited this language and the experience of this self-concept over many generations.

Your internal narrative can either empower you or limit you. If your inner film is a drama filled with self-doubt, fear, or negativity, then that's the energy you're going to bring to everything you do, and those are the experiences you're going to manifest. If your internal movie is filled with positivity, confidence, abundance, and joy, then that's the life you'll create!

Here's the most powerful part: you are the director of this movie. If you don't like the film playing, change the script, recast the characters, and shift the storyline. If you've been playing the role of someone who thinks she's unworthy or incapable—like I was for far too long—rewrite your script. Decide. Choose to be the hero of your own story, powerful in your own way, abundant, and capable of achieving anything you set your mind to.

Abdullah taught Neville that your imagination holds the power to change your life. Neville taught those who were ready to hear it that we all have a Divine spark within that has the power to shape our reality. If you can imagine yourself living the life you desire—enjoying a healthy body, being successful, finding love, achieving peace—then you can manifest it into your reality.

Changing your self-concept starts with a conscious decision to challenge and reshape your beliefs about yourself. Begin by envisioning your ideal self. Who do you want to be? Who were you born to be? How does this person think, feel, and act? Once you have a clear image, start aligning your thoughts, emotions, and actions with this ideal self. Believe in it wholeheartedly. Feel the joy and satisfaction of being this person in the depths of your soul.

One powerful technique is to live "as if." Start acting as if you are already the person you want to be. Feel the emotions you'd feel, and make the choices they'd make. This isn't about pretending or faking; it's about aligning your energy with the reality you want to create.

Changing your self-concept requires courage and persistence. But I promise you, as you begin to embody this new version of yourself, your external world will begin to mirror this inner transformation. Opportunities will present themselves. The right people will appear. Life will align in ways you can't imagine.

Your self-concept is a blueprint for the life you're creating.

Abdullah's success as an elder, immigrant, and dark-skinned Black man in his time period who was doing esoteric work is a testament to the impact a strong, positive self-concept can have.

Here's how to apply this scroll:

- **Believe your worth.** This is the foundation of a healthy self-concept and crucial for manifesting. When we believe we are deserving of good things, we align our energies with the outcome we desire, making manifestation our destination.
- **Challenge blocked beliefs.** Challenge any beliefs that hinder your manifestation process. If you perceive certain goals as unattainable, you may block your own path to achieving them or keeping them.
- **Visualize and act "as if."** Abdullah didn't just visualize himself in the orchestra seats, he acted "as if" it was already a reality. When it comes to manifestation, visualizing our desired outcome and acting "as if" it's already our reality brings that reality into existence.

- **Stay resilient and persistent.** Hold fast to your vision and continue to believe in it, even when faced with obstacles or delays.
- **Be patient.** Nurture your positive self-concept, visualizing your desires, and acting "as if," and you'll see your desired reality unfold.

What About Self-Love, Self-Esteem, and Self-Worth?

Self-love, self-esteem, and self-worth are all components of self-concept. They're like different facets of the same diamond, each playing a crucial role in shaping your overall perception of yourself.

Let's break it down:

- **Self-concept:** This refers to how you perceive yourself, including your beliefs about your own attributes, behaviors, and how you relate to the world around you. It's essentially your mental picture of who you are. This picture can be accurate or distorted, and it can positively or negatively impact your thoughts, emotions, and behavior.
- **Self-love:** This is the appreciation and affection you have for yourself, which includes taking care of your own needs, not settling for less than you deserve in relationships, and making time for activities that nourish and fulfill you. Self-love encourages you to show compassion toward yourself, to recognize your intrinsic value, and to treat yourself kindly.
- **Self-esteem:** High self-esteem involves believing you are capable, competent, and worthy, while low self-esteem reflects feelings of inadequacy or self-doubt.

- **Self-worth:** This represents the belief in your inherent value as a person. Self-worth is the recognition that you are deserving of respect, kindness, and positive life experiences, regardless of your achievements, failures, or what others might think of you.

Your view of yourself is influenced by every thought you choose to focus on. Pay attention to how you see yourself in all areas of your life. It shapes your future.

Seeing the World through Victim-Colored Glasses

Everything shifts when you realize that no one else is controlling your life. When you really get that you're the source of everything in your life and you have the power to create anything you want, how you see yourself shifts to a place where anything is possible. It's like finding a secret world where your potential is unlimited. (Because it is!)

An old friend—I'll call him Andrew—feels like everything and everybody is always against him. Andrew feels like life is constantly throwing problems at him, and he's just trying to get by. When you think this way, it seems like you're always getting the worse deal. The world seems unfair and you feel like you're always struggling.

This way of thinking makes you feel like you're controlled by things around you. For Andrew, family and business relationships of all kinds always seem disappointing and work feels like a constant battle. With his perception that "life is a struggle," he perceives himself as just reacting to life instead of creating it. He describes this as being on a boat without a steering wheel, tossed around by life.

Seeing the world as a victim also makes you pessimistic about the future. It's hard to imagine things getting better when you feel like you have no control. Expecting to be let down becomes a habit, trapping you in a cycle of negative thoughts that keep coming true. It's a self-fulfilling prophecy.

But here's the good news: just like you can choose to think of yourself as a victim, you can choose to think differently.

You're not controlled by what happens to you. You have influence in your own life. Slowly start to replace the idea of being a victim with the idea of being in control and watch how the world changes. With this new viewpoint, you're no longer just going along with what happens. You are actively shaping your own life.

Exercise: How to Shift your Self-Concept

If anyone tries to upstage you to make you feel little and he is big, make a mental image of him sitting on the toilet and you will bring him down to earth.

— *Abdullah*[2]

Purpose: To build a healthy self-concept.

Have you ever heard Abdullah's cheeky advice for when someone tries to belittle you? (I'm not British, but that's the only word that fit.) Now that's what I call a down-to-earth strategy, literally! When you see yourself as capable, deserving, and worthy of respect, other people will have less impact.

What to do:

1. **Practice self-awareness.** The first step to change is awareness. Reflect on your current

self-concept. Be brutally honest. Observe the thoughts that pop up. *Are there ways you see yourself that hold you back? Do you have beliefs about yourself that are negative or limiting?*

2. **Envision your ideal self.** Create a clear, compelling image of your desired self-concept as a guidepost for your journey. *Who were you born to be? How does this person behave? What kind of thoughts do they have? Who is in their life? What do they value?*
3. **Use affirmations and decrees.** Affirmations, mantras, declarations, and decrees are positive statements that can help you challenge and overcome negative thoughts. Write down affirmations that align with your ideal self and repeat them daily. Your brain believes what you tell it repeatedly.
4. **Act "as if."** Start acting "as if" you are already the person you want to become. This isn't about "fake it till you make it" pretending. It's about behaving in ways that align with your new self-concept. When you start to act "as if," your beliefs catch up.
5. **Surround yourself with positivity.** The people and environments you surround yourself with impact your self-concept. This is why creating healing and empowered communities like my retreats and online circles is a key part of my work. Seek out positive, supportive people. Spend time in environments that inspire you.
6. **Practice self-compassion.** Change is a process. Be patient with yourself. There will be setbacks and self-doubt. It's okay to stumble. Be nice to you.
7. **Get professional help.** If you're finding it challenging to shift your self-concept on your

own, consider professional help. A skilled therapist, counselor, healer, life coach, course, or community can provide valuable guidance and support.

8. **Repetition is power.** Your brain is designed to form habits through repetition. Regularly revisiting your affirmations, visualizing your ideal self, and acting "as if" helps your brain to establish new patterns. The more you repeat these behaviors, the more natural they become. Over time, your brain will accept your new self-concept as your reality. Think of it as creating a new groove in your brain that gradually deepens until it becomes your default way of thinking, feeling, and behaving.

Exercise: Manifesting through Identity Mapping

Purpose: To create a visual representation of your desired self-concept and use it as a manifestation tool.

Duration: One week

Materials needed:

- A large piece of poster board or paper
- Markers, pens, or colored pencils
- Magazines for cutting out images (optional)
- Glue or tape (if using magazines)
- A quiet space for reflection

What to do:

1. **Brainstorm your ideal self-concept.** Spend 15 minutes jotting down words, phrases, or ideas that represent your ideal self-concept in different

aspects of your life—relationships, career, health, spirituality, finances, leisure, et cetera.

2. **Divide the board.** Divide your poster board into sections that represent the different areas of your life where you want to improve or transform your self-concept.
3. **Build the sections.** In each section, write down or glue images that represent the ideal self-concept you wish to embody. This could consist of words of affirmation, pictures of experiences you want to have, or symbols that mean something to you.
4. **Add a central image.** Place a photo or drawing of yourself in the center of the board, surrounded by your ideal self-concept. This represents the "new you" that you are manifesting.
5. **View the board daily.** Spend at least five minutes each day looking at your self-concept map. As you look at each section, visualize and feel yourself embodying that ideal self-concept.
6. **Affirm and declare your self-concept.** After your daily viewing, state out loud: "I am effortlessly becoming all that I envision. I am the creator of my life experience."
7. **Take action.** Identify at least one action you can take daily that aligns with the new self-concept you're aiming to embody. Write it down and commit to doing it.
8. **Reflect.** At the end of the week, journal about your experience. Did your thoughts or actions shift in any way? Did you notice any changes in your external world?

Your Self-Concept Decree

I am worthy of my dreams and goals.

Today, I am the master of my destiny and the architect of my world. I am not a leaf blown by the whim of the wind. I am the mighty oak standing tall against the storm, unwavering in my conviction, unshakeable in my resolve.

I am worthy of my dreams and goals.

No longer shall I be addicted to self-doubt, the good opinions of others, or fear-based beliefs. Every cell in my body now pulses with courage and confidence.

My past does not define me, and my present is my magic carpet. I embrace every challenge as an opportunity to grow, to shine, to thrive. People like me shine. People like me win.

I am worthy of my dreams and goals.

Today, I recognize the power within me. I am bold. I am badass. I am unstoppable. Today, and every day, I rise and I shine. And so it is.

Your Self-Concept Journal Questions

- What are some beliefs about myself that have held me back? How can I reframe these blocked beliefs into positive, empowering ones?
- If I was living as the most authentic, empowered version of myself, how would I describe myself?
- How does my current self-image align with my goals and dreams?

THE MYSTERY OF THE SUBCONSCIOUS MIND

You have it. And if you do not sleep tonight in the possession of it, you are not doing what I have told you.

— ABDULLAH[3]

Are you aware that you possess a miraculous source of creative energy that can shape your very existence? This incredible gift is your subconscious mind, a part of your mind that you might not be aware of, but it influences every aspect of your being.

Abdullah's star pupils Murphy and Goddard were both cheerleaders harnessing our subconscious minds to affect reality. They both taught that your thoughts shape your life, although they approached this idea somewhat differently.

In Dr. Murphy's most famous book, *The Power of Your Subconscious Mind*, he taught that the subconscious mind is a powerful creative force that can be harnessed for self-improvement, health, and success. Murphy proposed that our conscious thoughts, beliefs, and feelings shape the reality produced by our subconscious. He urged people to change their thought patterns and be more positive in order to better their circumstances.

Neville believed that everything exists in your imagination and one should "assume the feeling of the wish fulfilled." He taught that reality is created by your imagination and that by changing your thoughts and mental images, you can change your reality.

So what is your "subconscious mind"?

Imagine an iceberg. The little tip poking out above the water—that's your conscious mind. It's all the thoughts, feelings, and choices you're aware of. But underneath the water, there's a huge part of the iceberg you can't see. That's your subconscious mind. It's a kind of storage room for all your memories, emotions, beliefs, and experiences. Even though you might not see it, it's always there, quietly shaping how you see the world, how you act, and even the life you live.

Your subconscious mind absorbs and stores every experience, emotion, and thought you've ever had, acting as a vast, limitless reservoir of your personal history. It operates around the clock, using its vast database to influence your behaviors and decisions.

Your subconscious mind does not judge or discriminate. It accepts every thought, belief, and assumption as truth. These mental inputs influence how you perceive and interact with the world, molding your reality.

The beliefs and assumptions held in your subconscious mind dictate your attitude, reactions, and your expectations of yourself and others. If you subconsciously believe that you're not good enough or that success is out of your reach, you might find yourself self-sabotaging or shying away from opportunities that could lead to your growth and success.

Most of your subconscious beliefs and assumptions were formed during childhood, based on the messages you received from your environment. As you grew up, they became solidified in your subconscious mind and continue to influence your life, often without your conscious awareness. But the good news? These beliefs and assumptions can be changed. Basically, don't believe everything you think!

Every thought you have sends a ripple through your subconscious mind, impacting your emotions, behaviors, and overall mental and physical well-being. A consistent pattern of negative thinking can lead to stress, anxiety, and other health issues. On the other hand, nurturing positive thoughts can enhance your mood, boost your confidence, and even improve your health.

What's empowering about this is that you have the ability to choose your thoughts. (I know it doesn't always seem like it!) By recognizing the power your thoughts hold, you can begin to consciously steer your thought patterns toward the life you wish to manifest.

Your mind and body are not really separate. Your subconscious mind forms a bridge between the two, channeling the power of your thoughts and emotions into physical responses.

Picture this: you're about to give a big presentation, and you start to feel your heart race, your palms sweat, and your stomach churn. These are physical reactions triggered by your thoughts and emotions—an example of the mind-body connection in action.

Now, consider the implications of this connection for your overall health. If negative thoughts and emotions can create stress responses, what impact could chronic negative thinking have on your body? Research shows that stress can contribute to various health issues, including heart disease, digestive problems, sleep disturbances, and more.[4]

Positive thinking can stimulate the production of chemicals that promote feelings of well-being, help manage stress, and support overall health. By nurturing a healthy mind, you're contributing to a healthier body.

Murphy's Mindful Manifesting

In her book *Confessions of an 83-Year-Old Sage,* Helene Hadsell, a fellow believer in the power of the mind, shares a story from Dr. Joseph Murphy. Helene was known for her incredible success in winning contests and sweepstakes with the power of positive thinking, focused intention, and deliberate manifesting techniques.

Here's the story Helene shared:

Once upon a time, Joseph Murphy, who would later become a prominent advocate of the New Thought movement, found himself in humble circumstances. His only source of income came from a local radio station, where he composed "Thought For The Day" inspirational messages. His modest earnings barely covered his basic needs, but Joseph had grand dreams. He longed for a home with a garden, a water fountain, and a recording studio to produce self-help tapes.

For five months, two weeks, and three days, Joseph secluded himself in deep contemplation and visualization. In his mind's eye, he would sit by the water fountain in his dream house and enjoy the serenity. With each meditation, he would add more details to his mental picture of the house: artwork, carpets, a library, and bedroom overlooking the Hollywood Hills. His thoughts became so vivid that he felt like he could almost touch the objects in his imagined home.

Then an attorney knocking on the door brought Joseph out of seclusion. A fan of his radio segments had died and left her entire estate to Joseph. This benefactor, whom Joseph had never met, was deeply moved by his daily radio messages.

"Are you ready to see what you just inherited?" the lawyer said as he drove toward Hollywood Hills.

Upon his arrival, Joseph realized that it was the exact home he had visualized—down to the smallest detail.

"I was in total shock. Not that my programming had come to fruition, but it took such a short time. EVERYTHING I had programmed for had manifested. I almost blew it after we entered the home, and I saw the circular stairs leading to the second floor and asked. 'Is there a soundproof room upstairs?'"

Joseph's description was so clear that the attorney asked, "Have you been here before? How did you know there's a recording studio upstairs?"

Joseph explained, "That's been a desire I have had for some time, making tapes of positive affirmations. I've found the majority of people have to read or hear something over and over before it sinks in. Listening to tapes repeatedly will help change their mindsets."

Joseph's focused visualizations and persistent belief in his dreams imprinted them onto his subconscious, which worked to manifest his desire in the physical world. When the opportunity arose, the Mystery of the Subconscious Mind drew Joseph to the circumstances that matched his internal images.

His inner Abdullah was proclaiming, "You are in Barbados!"

The subconscious mind is always listening. It takes your most dominant thoughts and feelings, as impossible they may seem, and begins to shape your reality to align with them.

Practices to Use Your Subconscious Mind for Healing

Mindful meditation, visualization, and positive affirmations are powerful for shifting the subconscious. You may also want to try:

- **Subliminal Messages:** These are messages (words or sounds) presented below the level of conscious awareness, which influence the subconscious mind. Audio tracks with subliminal affirmative statements can influence your mind and body.
- **Hypnosis:** Hypnosis can help you access the subconscious mind directly for deeper change. It can quiet the conscious mind and open the door to the subconscious, making it more receptive to new ideas and beliefs. I have found hypnosis so helpful in my own growth, transformation, and manifesting that I've been studying it.
- **Emotional Freedom Techniques (EFT) or Tapping:** EFT is another of my favorites that I use with clients, myself, and my family. This technique involves tapping on specific meridian points while saying specific statements. The goal is to shift energy, reduce negative emotions, and facilitate positive change.
- **Emotional Journaling:** This practice focuses on exploring and connecting with the emotions tied to your desires. How do you want to feel? Journal about the feelings you would experience when your desire is fulfilled, not the situation, just your feelings. This practice helps your subconscious mind align with these emotions.

Is Positive Thinking Positive?: Beyond the Stereotypes and Spiritual Bypassing

In the world of personal development and spirituality, positive thinking gets a bad rap. Some say it's too simplistic, a kind of Pollyanna view that ignores challenges. But let's set the record straight: Genuine positive thinking isn't about putting on rose-colored glasses or avoiding difficulties. It's way more powerful than that.

Nobody expects you to be positive all the time. Feeling your feelings is one of the most transformational things you can do.

True positive thinking is not about denying hardships or avoiding emotional pain. It's about acknowledging these challenges and choosing to focus on your capacity to overcome them. By feeding your mind with positive thoughts and affirmations, you influence the foundation of your subconscious beliefs and assumptions, and shape how you see and interact with the world around you.

Now, you might have heard of "spiritual bypassing," a term coined by psychologist John Welwood. Spiritual bypassing uses platitudes to skirt around potentially uncomfortable moments. You know the phrases: "Just stay positive," "Love and light," "Thoughts and prayers," or "Everything happens for a reason." These kinds of statements are roadblocks to emotional growth, turning surface positivity into an emotional avoidance strategy.

Authentic positive thinking is different. It's a facilitator not a barrier for your personal growth. True positive thinking isn't about ignoring problems or feelings. It's a cognitive tool that enables you to maintain an optimistic outlook, empowering you to face challenges head-on.

As I shared earlier, research backs this up. Positive thinking isn't just some "feel good" philosophy. It's a transformative practice that encourages you to confront challenges with self-belief and hope. It doesn't negate your pain or difficulties. It helps you navigate through them. Real positivity is fuel for growth, not a shield to hide behind.

Exercise: The Seven-Day Manifestation Journaling Challenge

Purpose: To imprint your desire into your subconscious mind and align your thoughts and feelings for quick and effective manifestation.

Materials needed:

- A dedicated journal or notebook
- A quiet space
- 15 to 20 minutes of uninterrupted time each day for one week

What to do:

1. **Choose your desire.** Pick one specific thing you'd like to manifest. It could be anything, but try to make it something believable (to you) yet challenging.
2. **Craft your leading affirmation.** Turn your desire into a powerful, positive affirmation in the present tense. For example, if you want a new job, your affirmation could be, "I am thriving in my dream job that fulfills and rewards me."
3. **Set your space.** Find a quiet, comfortable space where you won't be disturbed. Take a few deep breaths to center yourself.

4. **Visualize and feel your new circumstances.** Close your eyes and vividly visualize living your life with the desire already fulfilled. Engage all your senses and emotions. What do you see, hear, smell, touch, and most importantly, feel?
5. **Write it down.** Open your eyes and write down your affirmation on the top of your page. Describe your visualization as if you're writing a story. Describe your new life with as much detail as possible, living with your wish fulfilled. Dive deep into the feelings and emotions you'd experience.
6. **Repeat the exercise.** Do this exercise at the same time every day for seven days.
7. **Let it go.** Once the seven days are up, let go of your attachment to the outcome. Trust that your subconscious mind is already at work, turning your manifestation into reality.

The key here is emotion and repetition. Feel the emotions as deeply as you can each time.

Check back in with yourself after a few weeks to see how you're doing and if your perspective or situation has shifted in any way. Get ready to unleash the manifesting power of your subconscious mind!

Subconscious Synergy: Creating Your Reality with Love Languages and Learning Styles

I have had the honor of working with hundreds of people on birthing to their goals and dreams. Empowerment is never one size fits all. I'm not for everyone, but even with my soulmate clients, some of my offerings fit and others don't.

Some goddesses thrive on my livestreams and podcasts, but would never attend my high-level, intimate in-person retreats. There are lightworkers who engage deeply with my oracle decks but are not into my transformational courses. This diversity in preferences and responses has led me to explore how integrating love languages and learning styles could enhance manifestation.

When it comes to conscious creation, the modern manifesting movement tries to fit everyone into the same mold. After working with every personality archetype imaginable, I've found that manifesting with your love languages and learning styles can unlock effective results. Understanding your love language and learning style can enhance your ability to communicate with your subconscious mind. This creates a more receptive environment for manifesting.

Exercise: Manifesting with Your Love Language

Dr. Gary Chapman's book, *The Five Love Languages*, teaches that we all have unique ways of expressing and receiving love. Our unique love expressions can influence our subconscious patterns and, as a result, our manifestation practices. By incorporating elements from all love languages, we create a balanced approach, integrating emotional, spiritual, and physical aspects of manifestation.

What to do, depending on your love language:

1. **Words of Affirmation:** For those of us turned on by words, affirming your goals and desires out loud can be particularly powerful. This can reinforce your intentions in the subconscious,

making them more potent for conscious co-creation.

2. **Acts of Service:** Actions often speak louder than words. Performing vibration-raising acts of kindness or service, especially when aligned with your aspirations, is powerful.
3. **Receiving Gifts:** If gifts speak to you, use symbolic objects aligned with your goals, such as a coin to represent financial abundance or a heart-shaped stone for love. These act as reminders to your subconscious, reinforcing your planned path.
4. **Quality Time:** Spending focused time on your manifestation practices embeds your desires deeply into your subconscious. This intensifies the energy behind your intentions.
5. **Physical Touch:** For those who connect through touch, incorporating tactile elements into manifestation rituals can make your desires more tangible. Holding objects like crystals during meditation or engaging in grounding exercises can physically and symbolically link your desires to your efforts.

By recognizing and integrating your love language with your understanding of the subconscious mind, you unlock a more effective and personalized path to realizing your dreams.

Exercise: Manifesting in Your Learning Style

Purpose: To expedite your manifesting goals by learning to recognize and align with your primary learning style.

Modern manifestation tools and processes don't align with everyone equally. For example, vision boards are popular but don't click for everyone. The same goes for journaling, affirmations, and meditation. We all absorb and process information differently. Some are visual, others auditory, read/write or kinesthetic.

If one method hasn't worked for you, it's not that you're doing it "wrong." There may just be a different approach that aligns better with how you perceive and interact with the world. The Divine frequency speaks many languages, so finding your preferred dialect can make all the difference.

What to do, depending on your learning style:

- **For Visual Learners**: Create physical or digital mood and vision boards or immerse yourself in detailed visualizations. Imagining yourself vividly achieving your dreams, as advocated by Neville, can impact your subconscious. This approach uses visual imagery to embed your goals into your psyche.
- **For Auditory Learners**: Use spoken affirmations or listen to guided visualizations. Dr. Murphy's teachings about the power of repetitive affirmations backs up this approach. Hearing and speaking your goals can tune your subconscious mind towards your desires.
- **For Kinesthetic Learners**: Embrace physical activities like walking meditation, yoga, or dance (of any kind) to manifest your dreams. Physical engagement helps you embody your dreams, making them feel more tangible and real.
- **For Read/Write Learners**: Write down your goals and intentions. Dr. Murphy's emphasis

> on affirmations aligns well with writing them down to impress these intentions onto your subconscious. Reading and writing about manifestation techniques and success stories can also shape your vision.

Incorporating your learning style can make manifesting more effective. Find harmony between your natural alignment and the powers of the subconscious mind.

Your Subconscious Mind Decree

I am the master of my mind.

Today, I take back my mind, the silent architect of my destiny. I acknowledge and affirm my mind's infinite power and potential.

I am the master of my mind. I greet every negative thought as a visitor passing through, acknowledging its presence but denying its stay.

My subconscious mind is an open field, fertile and ready for the dreams I dare to dream. Every morning, I greet the sun of new beginnings with gratitude, affirming my abundance. Every night, I am confident that as I sleep, my subconscious mind continues to work, continues to build, continues to manifest.

I am the master of my mind. My mind, my ever-obedient servant, mirrors my beliefs, reflects my thoughts, echoes my convictions. It works tirelessly, shaping my world to align with my inner vision.

I am capable. I am worthy. I am powerful. My subconscious mind is my ally, my partner in this dance of life. Together, we move to the rhythm of success, to the melody of prosperity, to the beat of fulfillment.

I choose my thoughts with care, understanding their creative power. I am the master of my mind.

Your Subconscious Mind Journal Questions

- What common patterns keep showing up in your life that might reflect your subconscious beliefs? Where could these beliefs have come from, and how might they have influenced your choices and life experiences?
- If your fears and self-doubts were trying to teach you something, what lessons might they hold?
- Picture the best possible future version of you, living the life you've always wanted. What beliefs does this future self hold? How can you start to nurture these beliefs now?

THE MYSTERY OF WORDS

I am very proud that I am a negro.

— Abdullah

From the dawn of civilization, words have been our main tool for communication, expression, and yes, creation. Words have bound us into agreements (and disagreements), moved us in poetry, and inspired bloody revolutions. Words have an inherent energy. When we understand and harness that energy, words can reshape our realities.

As a writer, I love words. My love language is "Words of Affirmation." I remember seeing Dr. Maya Angelou discussing the power of words on *Oprah*. She said that she doesn't allow cursing in her home because the words get in the walls and drapes. She explained that she knew one day scientists would be able to measure the power of words.

Neville saw "scientists, doctors, lawyers, bankers, from every walk of life seek an audience with old Abdullah." Abdullah was always an esteemed guest whenever he was invited out and all of these dignitaries were honored that he made time for private one-on-one sessions with them in his home.

Exalting on the sphinx, Abdullah said, "It embodies the four fixed quarters of the universe. You have the lion, the eagle, the bull, and man. And here is man that is the head. The crown of that creature called the Sphinx, which still defies man's knowledge to unriddle it, was crowned with a human head. And look carefully at the head, Neville, and you will see whoever modeled that head must have been a negro. Whoever modeled it had the face of a negro and if that still defies man's ability to unravel it, I am very proud that I am a negro."

Abdullah insisted on being called a negro over the polite, accepted, watered-down term of the day, "a colored man," because words matter. Abdullah said that he "didn't want any modification of what God had made him."

Neville and Dr. Murphy both emphasized the pivotal role of words in shaping our internal and external lives. The impact of our words is not just about semantics but about the beliefs, feelings, and intentions they carry.

Think of a single word: love. Depending on your personal experiences and current state of mind, this word might bring up feelings from warmth and comfort to pain and regret. This emotional resonance is due to the collective consciousness and your individual experiences tied to it. Now, imagine the magnitude of power and potential when we consciously choose our words, and embed them with specific intentions and feelings.

Every word we speak casts a spell over our lives.

Vibrational Energy of Words

Everything, from the largest star to the smallest atom, vibrates at a specific frequency. Words are no exception. When we speak or think a word, it releases a certain vibration. Positive words, like "hope," "love," or "gratitude," send out uplifting vibrations. They can brighten our day and the days of those around us. On the other hand, negative words, like "anger," "fear," or "resentment," emit lower vibes, potentially dampening our spirit and those in our vicinity.

I was watching *Sesame Street* with my daughter and they mentioned the saying "Sticks and stones may break my bones, but words will never hurt me." Adults wanted to make us resilient against bullying, name-calling, or taunts, but as we knew then and know now, words do impact us. Words might not leave visible scars, but they can affect our feelings, thoughts, and actions.

The energy of a word isn't just based on its dictionary meaning but also on the emotion and intention driving it.[5]

When we speak words without genuine intent, they fall flat. A casual "sorry" might not mend bridges, but a heartfelt apology can heal deep wounds. An "I can" whispered with true belief is stronger than a shouted "I can't." Our words, whether thought or spoken, carry vibrations and intentions that either nurture or block our growth.

I have personally used affirmations to redirect my inner voice. Long before I learned from the late, great affirmation queen Louise Hay, Reverend Jesse Jackson's affirmations had me feeling important. When I was a kid, he ran for president. It was pretty cool and unique at the time seeing a Black man do that. I didn't know much about politics, but I knew I was "somebody." Obviously, I missed the privilege of seeing my fellow New York Bajan Guyanese goddess Shirley Chisholm run as it was before my time. Reverend Jackson had every elementary school kid in my neighborhood chanting his affirmation, "I am somebody." As an adult, when I volunteered for the Obama campaign in Harlem, we had a new affirmation to direct our steps: "Yes we can."

From ancient India's mantras and meditations to ancient Egypt's *heka*, or magical speech, the power of words transcends cultures. African traditions, like those of the Yoruba and Zulu, have priests and healers who invoke blessings through chants and rituals. The Nubians and the Dogon also worked with spoken words and belief. Native American tribes like the Lakota Sioux and the Navajo, along with the Maya and Shipibo in Central and South America, emphasize rituals that invoke chants for spiritual connections and healing. Meanwhile, The First Nations People of Australia invoke ancestral spirits through Dreamtime stories, and New Zealand's Maori people channel power via the Haka. Across these ancient systems, the spoken word serves as a bridge between human intention and the manifestation of reality.

So what does this mean for conscious manifesting?

Let's check out one of Abdullah's favorite books, the Bible.

"In the beginning was the Word, and the Word was with God, and the Word was God." (John 1:1).

This line from the Bible tells us something big: words are powerful. It's like saying that before anything else, there was a word, a sound, or a voice. And this voice had the power to create and change things.

Think about this line as well: *"Let the weak say, 'I am strong.'"* (Joel 3:10).

It's an affirmation, teaching believers to speak their desired reality into existence. It's like giving yourself a pep talk.

Throughout the old and new testaments, there are many moments when words made things happen. Like when God said, *"Let there be light,"* and there was light. Or when Jesus spoke, and miracles happened. These weren't just words; they were powerful actions.

Folks call Abdullah's teachings "new age," but they are an ancient secret that we're still learning about today.

Exercise: Your Auditory Imagination

Purpose: To learn how to use your senses for manifesting.

Words are not just read or written; they're also spoken and heard. The sound of words, the way they're spoken, and the context in which we hear them can significantly enhance their power for manifestation.

Manifesting effectively involves engaging all your senses. Visualization is powerful but the sounds we hear can evoke emotions and create atmospheres that are every bit as real as those we can see. Sounds, from spoken words to environmental noises, add depth and dimension to your mental imagery, making your desires feel real and emotionally charged.

To help you with this, here are three Neville techniques:

THE CONGRATULATIONS TECHNIQUE

- Identify your desire. Visualize it clearly in your mind.
- Imagine a close friend, family member, or colleague congratulating you on achieving your desired outcome. This person should be someone you trust and who would genuinely be happy for your success.

- Close your eyes and take a few deep breaths to center yourself. Then, create a mental scene where you're having a conversation with this person.
- "Hear" them congratulate you. Congrats! You're approved, a success, healed, a winner, accepted! Feel the warmth and excitement in their voice. Respond with gratitude and joy. Experience the emotions as if the conversation is really happening.
- After this imagined conversation, open your eyes and carry that feeling of joy and achievement throughout your day.

HEARING BEFORE SEEING

- Define your desired outcome. Make it clear and specific.
- Close your eyes and take some calming breaths.
- Imagine you are in a place where your desire is coming true. It could be an awards ceremony, a party, or any other setting that aligns with your desire.
- "Hear" the sounds in this environment that confirm your success: applause, cheers, or any other sound cues that align with your desired outcome.
- After you create this vivid auditory experience, start visualizing the scene. See the people, the surroundings, and yourself basking in the success.
- Hold on to this combined sensory experience for a few moments, feeling the emotions associated with it. When you're ready, open your eyes and bring that energy into your day.

EAVESDROPPING TECHNIQUE

- Determine your desired goal.
- Close your eyes, take some deep breaths, and relax.
- Picture a setting where others might discuss your success, like a coffee shop, office, or family gathering.
- Imagine you're overhearing a conversation between two people who are talking about your achievement with admiration and respect.
- "Hear" their words and feel the emotions they evoke in you. Allow yourself to feel proud and grateful.
- After a few moments of experiencing this imagined scene, open your eyes and carry that sense of accomplishment with you.

These techniques are powerful tools to help you align with your desires and bring them into reality. They engage multiple senses, making your imagination more vivid and tangible. Practice these methods regularly and combine them with real-world actions to manifest your desires effectively.

Here are some additional tips:

Practice active listening. Train your auditory imagination by actively listening to your surroundings. Pay attention to the subtleties in sounds around you, their rhythms, and the emotions they evoke. This will sharpen your ability to re-create sounds in your mind.

Use affirmations. Create personal affirmations related to your desired outcome. Repeat these affirmations aloud or in your mind with conviction. Feel the emotions associated with these words to make them permeate your consciousness.

Add music. Music has the power to evoke strong emotions and can be a strong tool for manifesting. Create a playlist of songs that resonate with your goals. Listen to it regularly, feeling the emotions associated with your desires. I created a manifesting playlist that you can access at womanifesting.com/playlist.

Add soundscapes to visualizations. Along with your usual visualization practices, incorporate background sounds that align with your desired outcome. For example, if you're manifesting a beach vacation, use the sound of waves as a backdrop to your visualization.

Create scripts with dialogue. Write down a script that includes a conversation between you and someone else (real or imagined) in which you discuss your success or the manifestation of your desires. Read it out loud or play it back as a recorded voice note, immersing yourself in the dialogue.

Engage other senses. When practicing the Congratulations or Eavesdropping techniques, engage your other senses too. What does the setting smell like? How does the environment feel? This multisensory approach can make your visualization more vivid and immersive.

Be open and receptive. Maintain an open and receptive mindset. Trust in the process and believe that the universe is working in your favor. Surrender to the flow of life, knowing that your desires are on their way to you.

Manifesting with your auditory imagination is an ongoing practice. Be patient and persistent, and enjoy bringing your desires into reality.

Why Repeat Stuff?

When you keep hearing or saying something, your brain starts to think it's important. Over time, this repetition sinks deep into your subconscious. It's like setting a favorite tune as your alarm—after a while, even if you hear it in the middle of the day, your brain thinks, "Time to wake up!" If you keep telling yourself, "I am confident," guess what? Your brain starts to believe it.

Say your positive phrase often. The more you do, the deeper it goes into your subconscious. When you're just waking up or about to sleep, your mind is super receptive. It's like the VIP entrance for your affirmations. Maybe say it every time you brush your teeth, or when you're waiting for your morning coffee to brew. Don't just mumble the words; really feel them. Imagine the confidence, or the calm, or whatever your phrase is about. Use the magic of scripting here. Write down your phrase a few times a day.

Exercise: Create Your Ideal Life's Script

Purpose: To create scripts for visualization and affirmation.

Manifesting your dreams requires more than just wishful thinking; it involves channeling your thoughts, feelings, and actions in the right direction. Two proven methods stand out: the vivid imagination involved in Mental Scripting and the concrete clarity offered by Written Scripting. Let's dive into this powerful blend, uniting the principles of Neville's visualization techniques with Dr. Murphy's affirmation approaches.

Scripting, whether in your mind or on paper, is about bringing your deepest desires to life. It's a method of communication with your subconscious and divine consciousness.

What to do:

1. **Set the scene (visualization).** Start by imagining a vivid scenario that represents your desired outcome. Whether it's landing your dream job or traveling the world, visualize yourself there, in the middle of it. Feel the textures, experience the sounds, and bask in the energy.
2. **Inject dialogue (affirmation).** Add affirmations or dialogues to breathe life into this scene. For example, if you visualize a lavish office, accompany it with affirmations like, "I am highly valued here, and my contributions make a difference."
3. **Turn it up with dynamic emotion.** Neville and Murphy both emphasized the role of emotion. As you visualize and affirm, fill the scene with authentic emotion—joy, gratitude, or excitement.
4. **Add conversations.** Go a step further and include dialogues, perhaps a congrats note or a celebratory call from a loved one.
5. **Add physical anchors.** Ground your mental scripts with a physical action—perhaps a hug or a fist pump, making the experience even more real.

Emotion and Feeling: Beyond Words

When you combine a strong emotion with an affirmation or visualization, it's a direct message to your brain and the Divine that you're serious about this desire.

So, how can we make sure that our words are deeply felt?

- **Visualization with Emotion:** When you visualize, don't just see the scene—immerse yourself in it. Feel the joy, the excitement, and the gratitude. If you're visualizing a dream job, feel the happiness of getting that job offer, the pride in telling your loved ones, and the excitement of your first day.
- **Speaking with Intention:** When reciting affirmations or doing any form of verbal manifestation work, avoid mindlessly repeating words. Say each word with intention, understanding its weight and significance. For instance, instead of just saying, "I am rich," really feel the prosperity flowing into your life as you speak.
- **Body Language:** Our body often reflects what we genuinely feel. When using affirmations or visualizations, ensure that your body language aligns. Stand tall, smile, and open up your posture. It can amplify your feelings.
- **Emotional Anchoring:** Think of a time you felt incredibly happy, grateful, or successful. Focus on that feeling. Now, every time you practice your affirmations or visualizations, bring back that emotion. Anchor your current practice with that powerful past emotion.
- **Gratitude Journal:** Gratitude naturally evokes strong, positive emotions. Maintain a daily gratitude journal. Before or after your affirmations, write down three things you're genuinely grateful for. This can elevate your emotional state.

Cancel! Cancel!

Yes, words matter and words are powerful. Some folks are so worried about negative thoughts that they immediately say "Cancel! Cancel!" when they catch themselves thinking or saying something negative. They hope that this will stop any bad energy from affecting them.

Some people think that if they have even one negative thought, it might come true. So they try really hard to only have positive thoughts, which can be exhausting. One negative thought isn't going to ruin everything. What matters more is the emotion behind what we say and think.

A better approach is to stay aware of your thoughts and feelings. When you notice a negative thought, instead of reacting with fear and trying to quickly erase it, calmly acknowledge it. Try to understand why you're having this thought and then gently redirect your mind to more positive thoughts. Be compassionate with yourself; it's perfectly normal to have negative thoughts. What's important is how you handle them.

Be curious with your thoughts. What do they want you to know? What are they trying to protect you from or teach you?

Abdullah emphasized the importance of absolute belief in your thoughts and words. It's something to strive for. But being overly anxious and terrorizing yourself over every word or thought is not healthy. Achieving absolute belief is about believing in your ability to manifest your desires, not punishing yourself for every negative thought.

Be kind and gentle with yourself as you upgrade your belief system. Dr. Murphy suggested that when you catch yourself thinking negatively, immediately replace the negative thought with a positive affirmation. Neville teaches a technique called "revision," which you can find later in the book. This is more than just canceling a negative thought. It's about revising it and replacing it with a more positive scenario.

I believe in the power of positive thinking. But instead of worrying about every negative thought, focus on the emotions behind your thoughts.

Your Words Decree

My words matter. I am not a passive witness in life's grand play. My voice possesses the strength to manifest, to summon realities, and to bring my dreams to life.

Every word I speak carves my intentions onto existence. My words matter, and I will use them with purpose, to paint happy portraits of abundance, health, and joy.

I guard my tongue. For I know my words matter, and they will echo hope, courage, and success.

My words matter. The cosmos tunes in when I speak, recognizing that my words matter. With every declaration, I send ripples into creation, turning the tide in my favor.

I honor my voice. My words matter, and they will mirror the world I choose, showcasing my spirit's resilience. Each word of affirmation builds my tomorrows.

In life's grand symphony, my voice is my anthem. My words matter, and with each utterance, I will not just communicate, but manifest, create, and proclaim the beauty of existence.

Your Words Journal Questions

- Reflect on a moment in your life when words (spoken by you or to you) had an impact, either positive or negative. What emotions did they evoke, and how did they shape your thoughts, feelings, and actions?

- Consider the narrative you internally repeat about yourself and your life. Are there recurring words or themes that limit or empower you? If you could rewrite this internal script, what would it say?
- Think about your most deeply held dreams and desires. What words of affirmations can consciously choose to support their manifestation?

THE MYSTERY OF FEELING

I have said all that I have to say.

— Abdullah

Forget what you've heard from pop culture or social media about manifesting. Let's dig into a fundamental principle that many misunderstand—how our feelings affect manifesting. Modern manifesting coaches emphasize the importance of "high vibes" and emotional alignment. That has value, but what Abdullah taught Neville is fundamentally different and much more powerful. Neville's teaching in his book *Feeling Is the Secret* is that our feelings and divine consciousness are the creators of our reality, not just by-products.

The term "feeling" here means that you assume the *feeling* of having your desires already fulfilled.

This is where both the Abdullah Paradigm and the Abdullah Paradox come into play. You must awaken and claim your "I AM" divine consciousness and walk in the truth that believing is seeing.

How does this work in practical terms? Think of your mind as a dynamic duo. There's your thinking conscious mind, where you make daily decisions like what to eat or wear, and your feeling mind, your subconscious, which operates in the background, influencing your actions based on your deep-rooted beliefs. Your conscious and subconscious mind need to work together to manifest your stuff. Thoughts are the car and your feelings are the gas. Together, they drive you to your dreams.

It always goes back to the Law. When you fully assume and believe that your desires have already been met, you're not just throwing wishes out into the world, you're reprogramming your internal software. "Updates" in your reality follow—new experiences, relationships, and opportunities that align with your feelings and assumptions.

The concept of "living in the end" is central to this. It's not a one-time event but a continuous state where you assume the feeling of your desires as already fulfilled. It's more than hope; it's conviction. Hope leaves room for doubt, while assuming the feeling leaves the unshakable belief in the realization of your dreams. Your relationships, your health, and even your perceived "luck" transform as a result.

Stay vigilant, though. It's easy to backslide into old mental patterns. When you find yourself drifting, re-anchor your thoughts and feelings into your desired state, because your subconscious doesn't distinguish between daydreams and reality—it only understands the language of emotion. Temporary emotional highs won't cut it.

What manifests your dream life are your genuine, deeply felt emotions. Focus on cultivating these emotions that resonate with the core of who you are.

And that's the real secret: aligning your thoughts and feelings not just to manifest isolated outcomes, but to become the person you were always meant to be, leaving your unique imprint on the world.

Fall in Love with Your Desire

How do you feel about what you are calling forward? Do you really believe that what you are seeking also wants you? Are you lukewarm about your desires? Or do you have a burning desire?

This is why the only question Abdullah asked Neville about his burning desire to go home to Barbados is, "Do you really want to go?"

As Neville put it, "We fail because we do not fall in love enough with an idea. We aren't, I would say, moved enough to want to be other than what we are. If I could get you to be completely in love with some state to the point where it haunted the mind, I could almost prophesy that you would in the not distant future externalize that state within your world. And the reason we fail we aren't hungry enough to change. For either we do not know the law or we haven't the urge or the hunger to really bring about the change."[6]

To make a dream come true, you have to really want it. Fall in love with the state of your desire fulfilled. Here's the tricky part—don't fall in love with the state of desiring it or lack, because you'll get stuck there. Fall in love with the fulfilled desire.

Sometimes we don't get what we want because we're not excited or serious enough about it. If you're fully committed to a goal and feel it to be already fulfilled, you'll make it happen.

How would you feel when your desire is fulfilled? When you start feeling different on the inside—more confident, more hopeful, or more determined—you'll start seeing those changes in your everyday life.

The Flip Side: What About Negative Feelings and "Low Vibes"?

Before we go deeper into the magic of feelings and manifesting, let's have a heart-to-heart about your mental well-being. If you're struggling with depression or other mental health challenges, please seek help from medical professionals. Conscious manifesting is powerful, but it's not a replacement for the care you might need. It is okay not to be okay all the time.

Also, let's be real: Avoiding your issues by diving into spiritual practices isn't the answer. Spiritual bypassing could lead to unhealthy habits, like numbing yourself or even addictions. Take time to really feel what you're going through, without judgment. Every emotion is a guide, a messenger that helps us tune in to what's happening in our hearts and minds.

For example, when you're grappling with grief—be it the loss of a loved one, the end of a relationship, or an opportunity—it's natural to feel emotions that aren't high vibe. Grief is a part of being human, and it doesn't make you any less skilled at manifesting. Allow yourself the space to mourn and heal, knowing that when you're ready, you can continue with a deeper sense of compassion and understanding.

For those of you carrying heavy stuff, like traumas or deep-rooted fears, please know it's okay to ask for professional help. Slapping on a "positive vibes only" label won't resolve all issues. True change comes when we're brave enough to face our shadow selves and work through the tough stuff, with the help of a therapist or counselor, if needed.

Now, what about those days when you're not on your A-game, when the good vibes are nowhere to be found?

Does that mean you're off the manifestation track? In a world bombarded by "#GoodVibesOnly," it's easy to think that the key to successful manifesting is only in walking around in a nonstop party. Don't get it twisted; Abdullah didn't preach that.

It's not just about the emotions you're feeling at this very second but about the overall assumptions and beliefs you hold. Negative feelings don't doom you; they're just part of your emotional landscape.

Unwanted feelings aren't roadblocks; they're signposts. They can point you toward underlying assumptions that need revision. Maybe you feel unworthy or believe that good things don't happen to people like you. These feelings alert you to beliefs that you can then change.

Don't brush undesired feelings under the rug. Use techniques like revision to shift the emotional tone of past events. You assume the feeling of the wish fulfilled by focusing on the positive outcome you desire. This doesn't mean ignoring the negatives.

When you find yourself in a funk, persistence is the key to create a shift. Keep revising, keep assuming, and keep the faith. The consistency of your assumption will eventually override the temporary setbacks.

Let's get practical. The next time you're down, try Neville's revision technique. Replay the day's events but recast them with a better ending or feeling. Maybe someone overlooked you for a project; revise that scene to one where you're chosen and excelling. Feel it deeply.

Or practice the "feeling flip." Identify an undesired emotion you're holding and find its positive counterpart. If you're feeling fearful about finances, what would financial security feel like? Assume that feeling. Sit with it, and let it override the fear.

The trick isn't to avoid negative emotions but to understand and transform them. In doing so, you're not just playing the game of manifestation better; you're becoming a more complete, self-aware individual.

Why Dominant Feelings Matter

I'm about to say the most Gen X thing ever: What if your emotional life was a playlist where each track represented a different emotion? Some would be upbeat, and others a little gloomy, but the songs you rock the most would be the defining soundtrack of your life. Your dominant emotions are the ones that resonate in your daily experiences and influence what you manifest.

But how do these dominant feelings become so influential?

You have the power to shape your own life. Your dominant feelings are important because they come from your assumptions or beliefs about yourself and the world. When you strongly believe or assume something to be true, you're telling your subconscious mind to make it your reality. Your subconscious then works in the background to bring about situations that align with these dominant feelings or beliefs. So, by consciously choosing what you assume or believe, you can steer your life in the direction you want it to go.

Here's how it works:

- **The Power of Persistence:** The emotions you dwell on become your reality. If your emotional state continuously vibrates at the frequency of love, abundance, and gratitude, then life brings you more of the same.
- **Lack vs. Abundance:** If your emotional playlist is mostly feelings of lack, unworthiness, or

negativity, you're basically requesting more experiences that confirm those beliefs. When your emotional state revolves around abundance and gratitude, you create experiences that resonate with those feelings.

- **The Cycle of Reinforcement:** What are you currently feeling into reality? Life continually gives you experiences that match your dominant emotional state. If you're locked into feelings of scarcity, you'll find that life only offers more reasons to feel that way. But, good news: this cycle is reversible. Once you shift your dominant emotional state to abundance, life starts mirroring those emotions back to you.

So how do you change the track that's playing on repeat in your life? Awareness is the key. Assess the following: *What has been my dominant emotional state lately? Is it aligning with what I wish to manifest?*

Consider keeping a "Dominant Feelings Diary" or section in your journal where you record the emotions you feel each day. Do they align with your goals and desires? If not, time for a change. When you catch yourself slipping into an emotional state that doesn't serve you, remind yourself of a time when you felt the way you desire to feel. Engage with that emotion until it returns.

The State Akin to Sleep (SATS): Your Gateway to the Subconscious

The State Akin to Sleep (SATS) is a powerful tool for infusing your dominant feelings with intent. SATS is that liminal space you enter just before falling asleep, where your conscious mind relaxes and your subconscious mind becomes more accessible. Neville and Dr. Murphy considered this a prime time to imprint your desires and shape your reality because the subconscious mind is exceptionally receptive in this state.

SATS is not just a gateway to your subconscious; it's when you can deliberately choose the dominant feelings you want to experience in your waking life. Your subconscious mind is nonjudgmental. It doesn't differentiate between what's "real" and what's imagined. So, when you vividly feel and visualize your desires during SATS, these emotions gain traction in your subconscious.

For example, if you're seeking a fun, sexy, and romantic relationship, use this special window of opportunity to imagine the feelings you'd experience sitting on a picnic blanket in the park, drinking champagne. Enjoy the rush of emotions of fulfillment, excitement, or whatever it is you expect to feel. Make these emotions your focus. You're placing a powerful emotional order with your subconscious mind.

What makes SATS work so well with your dominant feelings is its ability to embed these feelings into your subconscious. Remember, your subconscious governs a large part of your behavior and reactions. Influencing it means you're more likely to act and think in ways that align with your desires. This sets off a cycle where your dominant feelings, which are now securely planted, continue to be reinforced in your daily life. These emotions help manifest the reality you've been hoping for.

Prayer as a State of Receptivity

Instead of seeing prayer as a petition for what you lack, Neville frames it with Abdullah's teachings as an opportunity to resonate with the feelings associated with already having what you desire. Prayer becomes a deliberate exercise in tuning your emotional playlist to the frequency of your aspirations. By assuming the feeling of your wish fulfilled, you are setting your dominant emotional tone to one of "having" rather than "wanting."

Revision: Emotional Time Travel

Another tool you can use to alter your dominant feelings is The Revision Process. With this technique you to revisit past events and experience them with the emotions you wish you had felt at the time. Most of us spend time going over the past in our heads mulling over the things that made us unhappy, uncomfortable, or disappointed. Imagine reconfiguring your past, retroactively replacing regret or disappointment with joy or success. This doesn't just change your feelings about the past; it can also reset your emotional trajectory, influencing your future experiences and manifestations. You are replanting the seeds of emotion in the fertile soil of your subconscious, laying the groundwork for a reality that better aligns with your desires.

While these techniques are effective tools for manifesting, they'll be explored in more detail in the bonus processes section at the end of this book.

Exercise: The "Living in the End" Feelings Amplifier

Purpose: To program your subconscious mind to manifest your desired outcomes using your dominant feelings and the SATS technique.

What to do:

1. **Choose your sanctuary.** Find a quiet place where you can focus, free from disturbances.
2. **Choose your desired outcome** for something that you are manifesting. Close your eyes and visualize your desired outcome or imaginal scene in vivid detail.
3. **Dive into the emotion.** Immerse yourself in the emotion you would associate with your wish fulfilled.
4. **Turn up the volume.** Imagine an emotional volume knob in your mind. As you dwell on the emotion, gradually turn up the knob, letting the emotion swell and envelop you. The idea is to make this feeling the star of your inner world, allowing it to dominate your consciousness.
5. **Have a nighttime amplification session.** As you approach bedtime, remember this dominant, amplified emotion. In a relaxed state, let the amplified emotion be the last thing you experience as you drift off to sleep, seeding it deep into your subconscious.

Your Feelings Decree

My feelings create.

Within my soul, a force awakens. Today, I stand tall in this realization: my feelings have the power to sculpt my destiny.

My feelings have creative power.

With every pulse of my heart, I channel emotions of love, abundance, and joy, letting them light the path ahead. These feelings are my guiding star, leading me even during life's most turbulent storms.

When clouds of doubt loom overhead, I trust the innate power within me. For every emotion, whether of elation or despair, serves a divine purpose. They are the sacred messengers of my journey, steering me closer to my purpose.

My feelings have power.

From this moment on, I celebrate and honor my feelings. They are my compass, and my allies. My feelings are the key.

And so it is.

Your Feelings Journal Questions

- Recall a moment in the past week when you felt a strong emotion. What insights or revelations does this emotion reveal about your current path and desires?
- If your most dominant feeling from today was a seed for tomorrow's experiences, what would you manifest? Are you in alignment with this outcome? If not, which emotion would you prefer to amplify to shape your destiny?
- Think of a time when a seemingly negative emotion led to unexpected growth or change in your life. How did that emotion serve you, and what did it teach you?

THE MYSTERY OF STATE

You do not say "how" when you "are there." You are there. Now you walk as though you were there.

— Abdullah[7]

Your state is your emotional and mental environment at any given moment, and it reflects your deepest beliefs, feelings, and attitudes about yourself and the world around you. Pay attention to it because your predominant state creates your world.

The way Neville put it is, "Pick out a lovely state, go right into it and dwell there. I call that occupying the state and thinking from it instead of thinking of it."

This concept can be a challenging shift. So how did I get the magnitude of this state concept?

Let me take you on an incrediblel ride that includes a stadium, Tony Robbins, and, yes, real fire. Imagine standing in front of a bed of hot coals, the angry heat blazing toward you. Your grand plan is to walk—barefoot—across this fiery path.

Crazy? Maybe. Life-changing? Absolutely.

The Pre-Walk State

Transformational coach Tony Robbins hosts a semi-annual dynamic and transformative mega-seminar with 15,000 people from around the world. Firewalking is a part of the experience to symbolize the power of facing and overcoming deep-seated fears. Feeling stagnant, I decided to attend this empowerment event to challenge my boundaries and unlock new levels of personal potential. I lead international retreats because I believe in the power of guided immersive experiences.

Before attending the event for the first time, I experienced a mix of fear, anxiety, and skepticism. I gave myself permission to opt out at any time and then decided "Nope!" I wasn't going to do the firewalk. Fearful thoughts swirled in my mind: "This is dangerous. What if I get burned?" My focus was on potential pain, not on transformation. My body/physiology? Hunched shoulders and shallow breaths—clear indicators of a fearful state.

Shifting My Internal Gear

Then I got pumped up. I remembered who I was and whose I was. I embodied my "I AM" consciousness, the Abdullah Paradigm. I stood up straight, took a life-affirming deep breath, and shifted my focus from fear to the person I'd become once I made it to the other side. The language in my head and in my conscious and subconscious minds had changed from "What if I get burned?" to "I am unstoppable."

The Walk and the Shift

As I took that first step onto the glowing embers, something magical happened. Fear disintegrated. The fire under my feet, the distant cheers, and the beat of my heart merged into one symphony, one song, one verse. Universe. I was immersed in the experience, one with the spark. My ancestors were right there with me, feeling the heat, the exhilaration, the transcendence. I wasn't thinking of the next step; I was the step. Before I knew it, I had crossed to the other side, unscathed. My state had shifted from fear to limitless possibilities.

Walking on fire wasn't just an adrenaline rush. It was a lesson in understanding my state and capability to transform my entire reality. It was the embodiment of Abdullah's teachings on "assumption." I assumed a new state where fear had no stronghold over me, and that state manifested as an empowering experience that shattered my previous limitations.

My experience of walking across fiery coals was a tangible manifestation of the "feeling of the wish fulfilled." Just as Abdullah proposed to Neville, I adopted the feelings, beliefs, and attitudes of the new state before making the walk. I was already victorious, visualizing myself *after* walking across the coals unburned. I felt the joy, relief, and empowerment that would come after walking on fire, and I brought those feelings into the actual experience.

I transitioned into a new state and my external reality —in this case, those hot coals—had no choice but to conform to this new state of consciousness. I've done it a few times now and I see this fire walk as a metaphor for any challenge or desire I encounter in life.

The key to overcoming any obstacle or realizing any dream is to change your state to match the "feeling of the wish fulfilled." Once that's done, reality has to fall in line. The real challenge isn't the fire or the hot coals. The real challenge is the current state you're operating from. When you master your state, you master your world.

Let's Go Deeper

Imagine your state as a paint palette. Each color represents different feelings, beliefs, and attitudes. The painting you create—which is your life—depends on the colors you choose. If you dip your brush into the hues of love, abundance, and positivity, you manifest a vibrant, fulfilling reality. But if you choose shades of fear, lack, and negativity, life might feel a little gloomy.

Our lives are an endless journey of moving through different states. Everything you experience in your external world is a reflection of your internal world—your state. The world reflects the contents of your consciousness.

Say you're in a state of lack—you're constantly worried about not having enough. You might notice that reality seems to confirm this: opportunities seem scarce, bills pile up, and financial prosperity feels like a distant dream. Let's shift this perspective. Instead of seeing these circumstances as affirmations of your lack, view them as reflections of your current state. To change your reality, change your state.

"But how do we change our state? It seems like such a huge thing!" you might ask. And, yes, it can feel daunting. But it's also empowering. Because you hold the key to your reality.

To change your state, you change your feelings, beliefs, and attitudes. Shift your focus from lack to abundance, from fear to love, from impossibility to possibility. Move into a state where you feel and believe that your desired reality is already here. Immerse yourself in the joy, gratitude, and satisfaction that accompanies your fulfilled desire. And then watch as your external world begins to reflect your new state.

The Mirror Principle: Reflecting Your State

The great Sufi poet Rumi once said, "Yesterday I was clever, so I wanted to change the world. Today I am wise, so I am changing myself." To understand and appreciate the power of your state, let's look at a fundamental principle that Neville often spoke about: the Mirror Principle. Your world is a mirror that reflects your internal state.

As Neville said:

> Stop trying to change the world since it is only the mirror. Man's attempt to change the world by force is as fruitless as breaking a mirror in the hope of changing his face. Leave the mirror and change your face. Leave the world alone and change your conceptions of yourself. The reflection then will be satisfactory.[8]

What does this mean? When you look in the mirror, the image you see is a reflection of you. The mirror does not alter, judge, or resist. It just reflects what's in front of it in the same way the people we meet, the experiences we have, and the opportunities that come our way generally reflect our inner state without alteration or judgment.

If you look in the mirror and notice that a hair is out of place, you wouldn't try to change your reflection, right? No, you would fix your hair, and the mirror would reflect this change. If you want to change your circumstances, instead of only trying to manipulate the reflection (your external circumstances), alter the source—your internal state.

For example, what if you're in a state of loneliness? In this state, you might see the world as an isolating place, where connections with others are scarce. You may encounter people who seem indifferent or unapproachable, experiences that reinforce that forming relationships is difficult.

Still, this is not proof that the world is lonely. These are reflections of your state of loneliness. The world, being the faithful mirror that it is, reflects your feelings of loneliness back at you, creating experiences that align with your internal state. The mirror principle can sometimes be a tough pill to swallow because it places the responsibility of our experiences on our own shoulders, but it's also incredibly empowering. You hold the power to change your reality.

Now, if you shift your state from loneliness to connection and love, feeling it in your core, the world-as-your-mirror will reflect this new state. You might notice people becoming more approachable, opportunities for connection appearing, and better relationships forming.

The change starts within, and the world mirrors it back to us. By adjusting our state to reflect our desires—feeling loved, successful, and abundant—we change the reflection in the mirror of the world.

Changing your state isn't about willpower or forced positivity. It's about a genuine shift in your feelings and beliefs as a beautiful and empowering journey of conscious creation.

Changing Your State

The first step in changing your state is awareness. Pay attention to your feelings, thoughts, and reactions. Observe them without judgment. Recognize the state you're currently in. This can be difficult at first, as we often go about our day on autopilot, not noticing the feelings and beliefs that influence us. But with practice, you'll become more in tune with your state.

Once you identify your current state, accept it. Don't fight it or judge yourself for it. Acceptance doesn't mean you want to stay in that state, but it does mean acknowledging it as your starting point. You can't change what you don't acknowledge, so accepting your state is a crucial step.

Now comes the fun part: shifting your state. This is where the Law and assumption comes in. As you know, assumption is about assuming the feeling of your wish as already fulfilled.

If your desire is to feel more loved and connected in your relationships, don't wait for the world to provide more proof of this. Assume this feeling now. Immerse yourself in the warmth, joy, and security that would come with such fulfilling relationships. If you want to assume a state you are unfamiliar with, imagine it. Think about your unconditional love of a child or beloved pet. Let these feelings seep into your being until they become your natural state.

This shift in state isn't temporary. It's not something you do for a few minutes every day and then return to your old patterns. To change your state, consistently embody your desired feelings and beliefs to make them your new normal.

Shifting your state isn't always linear. There will be moments of doubt, where old beliefs surface and challenge your new state. That's okay.

Gently guide yourself back to your desired state. Remind yourself of your power to choose your state. Reaffirm your commitment to embodying your desired feelings and beliefs.

Here are some ways to shift your state. Add those that resonate to your daily practice.

- **Mindful Observation:** This exercise is about becoming aware of your current state. Start by taking a few moments each day to check in with yourself. Pay attention to your feelings, thoughts, and reactions. Notice your inner dialogue, the recurring thoughts and beliefs that often go unnoticed. Don't try to change anything at this stage; simply observe.
- **Journaling:** Dedicate a few minutes each day to write down your feelings, thoughts, and experiences. Over time, you'll notice patterns and recurring themes that indicate your underlying state.
- **The "I AM" Exercise:** Write a series of "I am" statements that align with your desired state. For example, if you want to embody a state of abundance, your statements might include "I am abundance," "I am deserving of wealth," "I am always creating prosperity." Repeat these statements to yourself daily. Feel the truth of these statements as you say them. Let them seep into your subconscious and start to shape your state.
- **Visualization:** Take a few moments each day to close your eyes and visualize your desired reality. Engage your senses. What can you see, hear, touch, taste, and smell in this reality? How do you feel? The more vivid your visualization, the more effectively it can influence your state.
- **The Pillow Method:** As you lie down to sleep, affirm your desired state to yourself. Just before sleep your conscious mind is less active, and your subconscious is more receptive. You could use your "I AM" statements or simply embody the feeling of your wish fulfilled. Hold this state as you drift off to sleep.

- **The Mirror Technique:** Stand in front of a mirror, look into your eyes, and affirm your desired state. Seeing yourself as you affirm your new state can reinforce the belief in your desired reality and accelerate the shift in state.

Common Misconceptions and Challenges in Mastering Your State

Misconception: It's about denying reality.

- **Understanding It:** Changing your state is not about ignoring or denying your current reality. It's about acknowledging your present circumstances and consciously choosing to shift your focus toward your desired reality.
- **Navigating It:** Embrace acceptance as the first step. Acknowledge your feelings and circumstances without dwelling on them. Use them as a foundation for growth toward your desired state.

Misconception: Positive thinking is enough.

- **Understanding It:** While positive thinking can help with shifting your state, it's not enough on its own. Real change requires addressing your underlying beliefs and feelings.
- **Navigating It:** Combine positive thinking with deeper emotional work. Use practices like visualization, affirmations and shadow work to embody the feelings and beliefs of your desired state.

Misconception: My reality will instantly change.

- **Understanding It:** Changing your state can lead to changes in your reality, but this isn't always immediate.

- **Navigating It:** Be patient and trust the process. Recognize that you're altering long-standing patterns and habits. Maintain your focus on your desired state, and allow the transformation to unfold.

Challenge: It's hard to believe my new state.

- **Understanding It:** Shifting to a significantly different state can seem unrealistic.
- **Navigating It:** Start with small, manageable shifts. Aim for states that are a stretch yet attainable from your current position, gradually building up to more significant changes.

Challenge: I keep reverting back to my old state.

- **Understanding It:** It's common to revert to old states, especially early in the process, as you're working to change deep-seated patterns.
- **Navigating It:** Show yourself compassion and patience. Understand that slipping back is part of the process. Consistently guide yourself back to your desired state and, over time, it will become more familiar and natural.

The State Manifestation Method: A Step-by-Step System

1. **Define your desire.** Your desire is the "what" of your manifestation process. What is it that you want? Be as specific and detailed as possible.
2. **Identify your current state.** Your current state is your beliefs and feelings about your desire. Be aware of your current state to understand what you need to shift.

3. **Craft your desired state.** Your desired state is the state of the wish fulfilled. How would you feel if your desire were already fulfilled? What beliefs would you hold? This is your desired state.
4. **Enter your desired state.** Utilize the techniques we've discussed earlier—visualization, "I AM" statements, mindful observation—to start embodying your desired state. Feel the feelings of your wish fulfilled.
5. **Persist in your desired state.** Persistence is key. Keep embodying your desired state, even if your outer reality doesn't reflect it immediately.
6. **Surrender the outcome.** Surrendering the outcome means trusting that your desire will be manifested in the best possible way, without obsessing over how or when it will happen.
7. **Recognize and celebrate the manifestation.** When your desire is manifested, recognize it and express your gratitude. This reinforces your belief in the process and makes it easier to manifest future desires.

This is not a one-time thing. Keep refining your process as you go.

Your State Decree

Today, I embrace the truth that I am the creator of my reality. I acknowledge that my current circumstances are simply reflections of my internal state, a state comprising my beliefs, thoughts, feelings, and attitudes. I accept this truth not with judgment, but with the wisdom of understanding that I have the power to transform my world by changing this state.

I consciously choose to align my thoughts, feelings, beliefs, and attitudes with my desires.

Love, prosperity, health, success, and harmony are now my natural state. I revel in this state. I carry this state with me, knowing it shapes my world.

Even if I don't immediately see results, I persist, grounded in the faith of my understanding. I am patient, for I trust in infinite wisdom and its perfect timing. I surrender my desires to the Divine, confident that it conspires in my favor.

Today, and every day henceforth, I embody my chosen state. This is my promise to myself. I am the master of my state, the creator of my reality, and the artist of my life.

Your State Journal Questions

- What are the dominant feelings, beliefs, and attitudes within your current state? How are they reflected in your current circumstances?
- Imagine yourself living in your desired state. What changes do you notice in your thoughts, feelings, beliefs, and attitudes? How does your life look different from the way it is now?
- Think back on a past situation when a change in your state led to a change in your circumstances. What did you learn from this experience?

THE MYSTERY OF VIBRATION

God is love, just love.

— Abdullah[9]

Everything is vibration. Look under a powerful enough microscope and everything is moving. Everything—including our thoughts and emotions—exists as energy that vibrates at specific frequencies. These vibrations are not just abstract ideas; they influence our experiences and shape our reality. As Reverend Michael Bernard Beckwith says, "Energy flows where attention goes." Or as Neville put it, "As you imagine, you vibrate and call forth that which you have imagined."

You ever seen a tuning fork or singing bowl played? I use them both for sound healing, for myself and others. When a singing bowl or tuning fork is struck, they vibrate at a specific frequency and create a tone that matches that frequency. When you give off a specific vibrational frequency through your state, thoughts, and emotions, you create and attract experiences and circumstances that harmonize with that frequency. In other words, like attracts like.

The vibrational frequency of your thoughts and emotions acts like a magnet, drawing to you experiences and circumstances that resonate with that frequency. By consciously adjusting our vibrational frequency, we can manifest the experiences and outcomes we desire. Aligning our vibrational frequency with our desired outcome makes it easier for that outcome to manifest in our lives. The beliefs held within the subconscious mind shape our vibrational frequency, influencing the life experiences we create.

Instead of asking, "What do I need to do to get what I want," ask, "Who do I need to be to create and be aligned with what I want?"

Stay High Vibe?

As we discussed in the previous chapters, "staying high vibe" can be misunderstood as silly positivity or impractical. Within the context of the Abdullah's Mystery of Vibration, there's a richer understanding.

Instead of hoping for an unattainable state of eternal happiness, let's think about the dance between thoughts, beliefs, emotions, and vibrational frequencies. Emotions span a natural spectrum.

We are talking about aligning your energy with your desired outcomes. This alignment is about recognizing that your emotional state influences the frequency you give off. This frequency then interacts with the world around you.

The goal isn't to maintain a constant facade of positivity or avoid challenges or negative feelings. It's to empower you as the deliberate conductor of your own vibration. You are being called to harness the energy of your emotions and thoughts to shape your reality. Harvard neuroscientist Dr. Jill Bolte Taylor famously gave Oprah a huge "aha moment" with the sentiment "be responsible for the energy you bring." Dr. Bolte Taylor explains that, "When a person has a reaction to something in their environment, there's a 90 second chemical process that happens in the body; after that, any remaining emotional response is just the person choosing to stay in that emotional loop.[10, 11]

Too Woo-Woo?

An interesting thing about vibration is the controversy surrounding it in some well-known works. Napoleon Hill's popular book *Think and Grow Rich* and the groundbreaking film *The Secret* both initially contained references to the concept of vibration. However, due to concerns that the idea of vibration would be perceived as too esoteric or "woo-woo," it was edited out of the final versions.

Still, both *Think and Grow Rich* and *The Secret* resonate with the Law of Vibration.

The funny thing is that this is all pretty scientific:

- Wave theory, which covers how sound and light move as waves, matches the concept of vibration in metaphysics, as both involve the way energy moves in patterns.
- Resonance, found in things like musical instruments and bridges, shows that when vibrations are alike, they strengthen each other.
- In quantum mechanics, particles aren't thought of as solid objects but as possibilities described by patterns called wave functions, which work like vibrational structures and impact how particles behave.
- String theory suggests that the basic building blocks of the universe are tiny vibrating strings, with each kind of vibration representing a different particle, showing how vibration is a fundamental part of how our reality works.

The Vibrational Frequency of Thoughts and Beliefs

The same way that certain songs can evoke specific emotions, your energy vibes draw in experiences that resonate with your thoughts and beliefs. Just like different sounds have different pitches, each thought and belief carries its own unique "vibe" or energy frequency. These vibes are like messages that interact with the world around us and shape our experiences. You're playing your own unique song in the big concert of life.

The cool thing is that you can change the station! You have the power to shift your thoughts and beliefs to create different energy vibes. When you focus on positive thoughts, imagine your goals coming true, and believe in good things, you're tuning in to a higher-energy channel. This higher vibe creates experiences that match your positive energy.

Exercise: Practical Ways to Elevate Your Vibration

There's no rush on this path. You are worthy, and your desires are within reach.

- **Awareness:** Start by gently noticing how you feel right now. It's okay; there's no judgment here. Simply become aware of your current emotions and the thoughts behind them.
- **Gratitude:** Every day, take a moment to reflect on the things you're grateful for. This simple practice can uplift your spirit and open the door to positive energy.
- **Visualization:** Close your eyes and imagine your dreams coming true. Feel the joy, see the details, and let this vision fill your heart with excitement.

- **Affirmations:** Create affirmations that resonate with your heart's desires and repeat them with love and conviction. These positive statements can gently shift your beliefs over time.
- **Meditation:** Find a quiet space, sit comfortably, and let go of the outside world for a few minutes. In this peaceful space, connect with your inner self and let your vibration naturally rise.
- **Surround Yourself with Positivity:** Choose to spend time with people who encourage your dreams and inspire your soul. Your environment plays a significant role in your vibrational frequency.
- **Physical Well-being:** Lovingly care for your body through nourishing food, movement, and rest. A healthy body provides a nurturing foundation for a higher vibration.
- **Breathwork:** Take a moment to breathe deeply, inhaling positivity and exhaling any tension or negativity. Your breath is a powerful tool for raising your vibration.
- **Release Resistance:** Trust in the flow of life. Let go of any resistance and embrace the adventure with an open heart. Know that the Divine is conspiring to bring your desires to fruition.
- **Practice Self-love:** Treat yourself with the same love and kindness you offer to others. Embracing self-love is a beautiful way to elevate your vibration.

Your Vibration Decree

With every heartbeat, I vibrate easily with the energy of creation.

I choose beliefs that resonate with success, abundance, and positivity. These frequencies are echoed back to me in the form of harmonious manifestations.

I wield my imagination to craft a life rich with color, texture, and vibrancy.

I resonate with the symphony of creation. In moments of joy, gratitude, and serenity, I create a resonance that aligns with my desires. And when challenges arise, I acknowledge their lessons, transmuting their energy into growth and understanding.

In gratitude for this knowledge, I declare my intentions with the vibration of a thousand voices, echoing in harmony throughout time and space. Today and every day, I affirm that I am a master of vibration, a conductor of energy, and a creator of my destiny.

And so it is.

Your Vibration Journal Questions

- How can you consciously shift your vibrational frequency to attract and create more positive and aligned experiences?
- What beliefs and thought patterns might be blocking your manifestations, and how can you shift them to vibrate with your desired outcomes?
- What daily rituals or habits can you cultivate to align your vibrational frequency with your desires?

THE MYSTERY OF LIVING FROM THE END

Did I see you in Barbados, the man you are, going third class?
You are in Barbados and you went there first class.

— *Abdullah*

So I tried to open up my discussion with Abdullah, and I said, "Ab, I did all that you told me. I clothed myself with Barbados, I am sleeping in Barbados, and yet here I am in New York City." He would not talk to me. He turned his back upon me the very first time I brought it up; he walked towards his studio and slammed the door in my face. And if you knew Abdullah as I knew him that was no invitation to come in.

— *Neville*[12]

Bam! Door slam. Slam the door on doubt and disbelief. Bam! Door slam. Slam the door on fear and insecurity. Bam! Door slam. Slam the door on distractions and negativity.

"Living from the end" means behaving as if you already have what you want, even if it hasn't happened yet. You fully believe in and feel what it's like to be the person you want to be, or to be in the situation you want.

Neville tried to do this by pretending he was already in Barbados in his mind. When he started doubting this, Abdullah didn't say anything. He simply turned away and closed the door. This was his way of telling Neville to keep believing he was in Barbados, even if it didn't seem true.

"Living from the end" is a powerful way to manifest your desires. When you believe and feel like you've already got what you want, you start thinking, feeling, and acting like it's true. Your higher self then co-creates your desires with The Divine, infinite field of energy. That is the Law.

It's not enough to just imagine what you want. You have to fully believe it's already yours. Keep living as if you've already got what you want, even when it doesn't look like it's happening.

We're on to something magical here!

Picture this: You want to get fit and healthy. Instead of focusing on the struggle of the process or the distance you still have to go, you begin to live as if you've already reached your fitness goals. As a person who is already healthy and fit, you celebreate every workout, and eat vibrant, nourishing food as if it's the fuel for your perfectly healthy body. You look in the mirror and see a healthy, fit person looking back at you. You're living in the end of your fitness ideal, and it feels wonderful.

Or let's say you're dreaming of a promotion at work. Instead of stressing over every hurdle in your path, you start to embody the role you desire. You take on projects with the confidence of someone who already holds that position. You move, speak, and interact as if you're already at that level. You dress the part, think the part, and feel the part. Before you know it, you're no longer chasing the promotion. The promotion is chasing you!

Living in the end means you're not just picturing your dreams but feeling and acting as if they've already come to fruition. It's about aligning your thoughts, feelings, and actions with your desired reality. And this, my friend, is where good juju happens!

Let's circle back to the power of your imagination. You'll recall that we discussed imagination as not just a playground for the mind, but a divine tool of creation. Imagination is like a magic wand for making things happen. Imagining creates an inner blueprint for manifesting.

The Power of Secrecy

Incorporating sacred secrecy into Living from the End can accelerate manifestation. By privately holding your vision, you create a personal, sacred space for your dreams. This aligns with Living from the End, as it lets you fully embrace your goals without external interference. This created a stronger, undisturbed connection with your desired outcome.

Delve into John McDonald's book *Message of a Master* and you'll notice a familiar voice that might remind you of Abdullah's teachings. McDonald, with strong evidence, is rumored to be an Abdullah student and McDonald's Master is suspected to be an homage to Abdullah, a wink across the pages of history and spiritual empowerment. Like Abdullah, McDonald's "Master" challenges and provokes to unlock that dormant power within us, showing us the threads between beliefs and reality.

The book tells the transformative story of a man who encounters a mysterious, enlightened figure known as the Master. The book emphasizes the connection between our inner world and external reality, highlighting the significance of faith, visualization, and purposeful action in manifesting.

In the book, the Master says it's best to keep your dreams and goals to yourself until you achieve them. He thinks that talking about them too early can drain your energy and make it harder to reach them. Plus, sharing might invite negative comments or doubts from others, which could bring you down. Some people might even push their own fears onto you, making you doubt yourself. The Master believes that by keeping your plans private, you can focus better and avoid negativity. This idea might sound different from today's belief in sharing goals to stay accountable. When I was going through IVF, I didn't tell many people in my life because I didn't feel emotionally strong enough to hold my belief in the face of their judgement or crticism.

The power of secretness is about nurturing a relationship with your inner self, where your desires are protected, believed in, and manifested without being diluted by external voices. When you honor your inner sacred space, you magnify your manifesting.

Embracing the Concept of "Assuming the Feeling of the Wish Fulfilled"

Think of a vivid, sensory-rich daydream where you're not just watching a movie, you're in it, living and experiencing every moment. It's better than virtual reality—it's reality. You're embodying the joy, the gratitude, the satisfaction—every emotion that comes with the realization of your desire. In doing so, you're impressing these feelings onto your subconscious mind, which accepts them as reality. This is assuming the feeling of the wish fulfilled.

Why is this so powerful? Because your subconscious mind can't distinguish between real events and vividly imagined ones. Ever seen a movie or news story that you couldn't shake? By assuming the feeling of your wish as already fulfilled, you're aligning your subconscious mind with your conscious desires, setting the stage for manifestation.

By now you know that visualization is a powerful tool to influence your subconscious mind, and the best example of this comes from the world of top performers. Picture astronauts preparing for space or Olympians gearing up for the gold—they all harness the power of visualization. They understand that the subconscious mind—the part of your mind working behind the scenes—can't really tell if what you're imagining is real or not. So, these astronauts and athletes teach their subconscious minds that success is imminent. This fuels their actual performance.

Exercise: Feel It Real

Purpose: To supercharge your manifesting by inviting your emotions to the party.

Emotions are the language that your body and the divine mind of the Universe understand. When you feel the reality of your dreams, you're not just painting a picture; you're stepping into it, you're living it, and you're making it real.

So why is it so important to incorporate feelings into visualization? Well, feelings are like the secret sauce that gives life to our dreams. They provide the energy that drives our thoughts into reality. When you pair strong, positive emotions with your visualization, you amplify the signal you're sending out. It's like saying, "Hey, this is not just something I want, it's something I already have, and it feels incredible!"

Now, how can we make this jump from just visualizing it to feeling it for real?

What to do:

1. **Create your sacred space.** Find a quiet, comfortable place where you won't be disturbed. This is your manifesting sanctuary.
2. **Relax.** Close your eyes, take a few deep breaths, and let your body relax. This calm state is the launchpad for your manifesting.
3. **Visualize.** Bring to mind the reality you want to create. See it in vivid detail. What does it look like? Who is there with you? What are you doing? The clearer the image, the better.
4. **Invoke your emotions.** Now, here's where the magic happens. Shift your focus from what your dream looks like to how it feels. If you're visualizing your dream business, feel the excitement of creating a successful project or the satisfaction of leading a team. If it's a new home, feel the joy of hosting friends, the comfort of your cozy Zen den. Fully immerse yourself in these emotions.
5. **Believe and live in your reality.** Hold on to these feelings even after your visualization session. Go about your day as if you are already living your dream. This is what it means to "feel it real."

Exercises: Practice "Living in the End"

Purpose: To learn how to tap into your imagination, evoke the powerful feelings that result, and live in the end.

What to do:

- **Guided Visualization Exercise:** Here's a simple process to get you started: Find a quiet, comfortable place and close your eyes. Take a few deep, relaxing breaths. Imagine your desired outcome in detail. What does it look like? Who is there? What are you doing?

  Now, shift your focus from what it looks like to how it feels. If it's a new home, feel the joy of moving in, the excitement of decorating each room.

  Stay in this state of fulfilled desire for as long as you can. The more you practice, the easier it will become.
- **Journaling Exercise:** Here's a prompt to get you started: "Today, I lived my dream of . . . It felt so wonderful when . . ."

  Fill in the blanks with your desire and how it felt when you achieved it. Write in the present tense, as if it's already happened. The key here is to relive the feelings associated with your wish fulfilled.

- **Role-Playing Your Future Self:** This exercise will help you embody the feeling of living from the end. It's a bit like acting, where you get to play the leading role in your own life.

1. Choose a specific time frame—perhaps an hour or a whole day—during which you will fully act as if your desire has already manifested.

2. Prepare a few props or items that signify your success. For example, if you're manifesting a new baby, set up her diaper bag you're going to need.

3. During the role-play, interact with your environment and people around you as if your wish has already come true. Speak the language, display the emotions, and make the decisions that your future self would make.

4. Observe how others respond to you and make mental notes of the shifts in your own mindset and confidence.

5. After the role-playing session, take some time to reflect. Did you discover any new feelings, thoughts, or behaviors that align with your end result? Make these a part of your daily routine.

This juicy method will not only help you practice "living in the end," but it also will give you a clear vision of what life will be like when you manifest your desires. The more you can make this role-play a regular part of your routine, the more natural it will feel to live from the end.

The Role of Patience, Trust, and Faith: Learning to Wait and Believe

When you're trying to make your dreams come true, it's natural to ask, "When will this happen? Why isn't it here yet?" We're all impatient sometimes, but manifesting often takes time. Think of it like a dance: you've got to know when to lead and when to step back.

Patience here doesn't mean just sitting and waiting. If you plant a seed, you don't dig it up every day to check if it's growing. You water it, give it sunshine, and let it do its thing. It's the same with your dreams. After you've imagined your future and felt the feelings that come with it, you have to give your dreams a chance to come to life.

Trust and faith is about believing it's all going to work out, even when you can't see any signs yet.

So how do you stay patient and keep trust alive when things aren't happening as fast as you'd like?

Here are some tips:

- **Be in the now.** Life is happening right this moment. Mindfulness helps you appreciate the present and can make the wait easier. Trust that things are unfolding as they should.
- **Say thanks.** Gratitude helps you focus on what you already have, not just on what you're waiting for.
- **Celebrate little wins.** Your big dream won't happen all at once, but lots of little good things will happen along the way. Enjoy them! They'll make you more confident that the big things are coming too.
- **Stick with it.** Keep up with your practices for imagining your future and feeling those good feelings.
- **Detach.** Stop trying to control everything and just trust that the Divine has your back. Letting go opens up space for good things to come into your life.

Patience and trust might seem like they're all about waiting and hoping, but they're actually powerful forces that help make your dreams a reality. So have faith in you and hang in there! Your dreams aren't just possible; they're on their way.

Potential Pitfalls and How to Overcome Them

Let's look at some common pitfalls when trying to "live in the end":

Doubt Creeping In: Your conscious, rational mind loves to question things. It might start whispering doubts like, "Is this even possible? Am I just fooling myself?"

- **Solution:** Doubt is just fear in disguise. It's natural and happens to everyone, even the most successful people. When you immerse yourself in the feelings of your dream fulfilled, doubts tend to fade away.

Struggling to Visualize: You might find it challenging to visualize or "feel it real." You might struggle to create vivid images or conjure up the associated emotions.

- **Solution:** If this is the case for you, try different approaches. Maybe writing down your dreams or creating a vision board might work better for you.

Neville was an artist and performer, so acting "as if," visualizing, and seeing from the end were all in his wheelhouse. The key is to find a method that allows you to connect deeply with your desired reality. Check the Bonus section at the end on manifesting with your love language or learning style.

Impatience: We live in a world of instant gratification. We might feel impatient when our dreams don't manifest instantly.

- **Solution:** Keep doing your practices, stay grateful for the present, and know your dreams are unfolding.

Observing the Current Reality: Sometimes, our current reality may seem so far from our desired one that it's hard to believe in our dreams.

- **Solution:** See the next section.

Blocked by Current Reality? Slam the Door on Doubt!

Listen up! You've been tiptoeing around your current reality like it's some permanent fixture. It's not.

What you're facing now isn't the end-all-be-all. It's just a blip on the radar, a temporary stage. Stop giving it more power than it deserves. Time to slam the door on doubt and uncertainty and step into your power like never before.

Got challenges? Obstacles? Who doesn't! But here's the no-nonsense truth: if you're not living in the end, you're not really living at all. You've got to believe that your dreams are already your reality. Don't just half-commit to this; go all in. The world outside might be shouting "impossible," "not yet," or "maybe someday," but you need to be your own loudest voice saying, "It's already done."

Got roadblocks? Use them as stepping stones. You think setbacks are there to derail you? Think again. Every single obstacle is a chance for you to demonstrate just how much you want what you're consciously manifesting. So don't crumble; elevate. Refine your focus, tighten up your beliefs, and charge forward.

This isn't the time for half measures or wishy-washy faith. Your dreams aren't going to wait for you to feel "ready." They're waiting for you to claim them, right now, by brazenly living in the end and trusting the process wholeheartedly.

You got this. Now go out there and act like it. Slam the door on anything that tells you otherwise. The only thing standing between you and your dreams is the story you keep telling yourself about why you can't have them. Tear that up and throw it in the trash. Write a new story where you made it happen.

Now get to it!

Door slam.

Your Living-from-the-End Decree

I am the master of my destiny.

Today, I shape the reality of tomorrow by living my desired future now. I am not merely a dreamer, but a visionary living the dreams of my tomorrow today. I walk, talk, and breathe in the glow of my fulfilled desires. I rejoice in the power of my imagination, painting a vivid picture of my future that I live in the present.

With every breath, I align myself to the life I desire. With every heartbeat, I affirm the truth of my wishes already fulfilled. I see my desired outcomes not as distant dreams, but as a present reality, like a traveler who has already arrived at his destination.

As I rise with the sun, I live my day in this blessed reality. I am victorious not just at the end but also throughout the journey, for I live from the end, transforming every moment into a celebration of my fulfilled desires.

This is the truth I hold. This is the power I wield. I am the master of my reality, living my dreams from the end, ever confident, ever victorious.

I am living my dreams, from this moment forward.

Your Living-from-the-End Journal Questions

- If you knew that your dreams were guaranteed to come true, how would that shift your actions?
- How would your daily life change if you were already living in your desired future?
- Think of something you're manifesting. How would someone who has already manifested this goal behave, think, and feel? How can you incorporate these behaviors, thoughts, and feelings into your life now?

THE MYSTERY OF THE OPERANT POWER

You do not know who he is.
Neither does he remember who he is. If you only
knew who he was you would sit right now at his feet.

— *Abdullah*[13]

"THANK YOU . . . GOD-IN-ME!"
"THANK YOU . . . GOD-IN-ME!"
"THANK YOU . . . GOD-IN-ME!"

The year was 1975. Abdullah was physically long gone. Neville had died in 1972. Dr. Murphy was preaching at his Church of Divine Science in Los Angeles.

The country was coming out of a recession. The World Trade Center twin towers were a new marvel. It was the disco era, but somewhere in the Bronx hip-hop had already jumped off.

The charismatic Reverend Ike, a student of Neville's,[14] stands bouffant-coiffed and James Brown-sharp at the pulpit in Washington Heights's grand United Palace. His "palace" is an extravagant former Loew's movie theater transformed into a cathedral for his 5,000-strong and ever-growing New York congregation.

"God is in you," he declares.

The congregation's response is immediate and electric: "THANK YOU . . . GOD-IN-ME!"

"THANK YOU . . . GOD-IN-ME!" is more than just a basic church call and response. It's an affirmation and acknowledgment that they embrace their own power. They're not thanking an external God. They are thanking their inner divinity as the source of power to consciously manifest their lives.

Reverend Ike teaches his students to pray head held high instead of bowed. God isn't distant; God is right there, inside each of them. It's a soul-deep realization. The power they seek is already within, waiting to shine.

They are the operant power.

While his predecessors laid the foundation, Reverend Ike used that ole razzle-dazzle and innovative media presence to bring his, Neville's, and Abdullah's principles to a wider, predominantly Black audience. He made history in 1971 by filling Madison Square Garden with believers. By 1973, he broke new ground as the first Black religious leader to host his own TV show, *The Joy of Living*. By 1975, he had more than 1,700 radio stations broadcasting his daily messages, and his taped sermons reached millions. When he outgrew Harlem's Sunset Theater, right down the block from where I would live decades later, he took over the Loew's theater and christened it his "United Palace," where he sat on an actual throne.[15]

I only recently started listening to Reverend Ike because I had heard so many disparaging things about him. Watching him now, I find it amazing how much I am his spiritual daughter. The parallels between his mission and my weekly livestreams is astounding. We even say some of the same affirmations.

Each "THANK YOU . . . GOD-IN-ME!" was a loud acknowledgment that the power to manifest a life of happiness, health, and prosperity is within.

Critics found him blasphemous. He replied, "If you are looking for a god-in-the-sky to depend on, if you are looking for a god outside of you to help you, forget it! God is within you. And when you discover God, you will discover Him within your own being."[16]

He encouraged his followers to "unlearn" the limitations that society and life had imposed on them. "Unlearn sickness and know health. Unlearn poverty and know prosperity."[17] To manifest this new life, Reverend Ike advised them to "decide" and "Be choosy. Know what you want. Say what you want. When you speak, be very definite."

Reverend Ike and his Science of Living were quite controversial. His preaching on prosperity and his flamboyant lifestyle, complete with multiple Rolls-Royces, raised eyebrows and sparked debates. Neville's seminars had been quite expensive so he appealed to a wealthier audience. Many in Reverend Ike's audience were newly successful, but he also encouraged donations from everyone including the poor, no coins welcome.

I asked one of my elderly Harlem neighbors about Reverend Ike, and he said, "Oh, they were just mad that he was putting us on, telling us how to get ours. Nobody wanted us knowing our own power and hearing that we are God. He didn't regard the poor as poor. *They* wanted the poor to stay poor."

Reverend Ike said: "Separate the truth of a person from what he appears to be. Look all the way through what appears, and see him, his Divine Self, the Presence of God within him. See him as he really is. There is only one true identity, and that is the Divine Self."[18]

You are the operant power.

— NEVILLE[19]

The biggest lesson Abdullah taught that echoes through the work of all of his known students and their disciples is that we are Divine and that our mission is to awaken the God-force within.[18] Or the way Neville put it:

> The first principle is: "Be still, and know that I am God" (Psalm 46:10, NIV). No matter what happens, turn within and be still. Know that your awareness is God and that all things are possible to you. Test yourself and you will prove this statement in the testing; then you will be free from your former limitations of belief.[20]

You are the operant power. What does that mean? You hold the operating keys to your own success, prosperity, and spiritual well-being. It's the Abdullah Paradigm.

Whether you are sipping your morning tea or drifting into dreamland, the captain, the sole sovereign of your life, is none other than you.

Reflecting on my life, I see lots of instances of blame, guilt, and victim consciousness. I blamed my mother for not understanding me, my father for being absent at times, my exes for broken promises, my doctors for misdiagnosing me, my childhood neighbors for making me feel like an outsider. I held grudges against my 5th grade math teacher for making me dread numbers, and my high school rivals for making me self-conscious about my skin color.

Yes, all those things did happen, but today I choose a different perspective.

I harnessed the healing power of forgiveness to dissolve past wounds. I revised and redefined those painful experiences as stepping stones. I don't need to wait for someone else fix things.

I am creating my life, moment by moment, thought by thought, belief by belief. And you can do the same!

Ye Are Gods

Capital G, God, the infinite, the absolute, the ultimate source of all creation, crafted us as splendid reflections. God poured into us, bestowing us with a divine gift—sovereignty. We aren't just passing through this life as spectators. No, my love, we are active participants, holding the force of creation within us.

But here comes the twist: We are gods, with a small g. Don't take this lightly, because this is not about egos. This is about the divine force active within each one of us.

My dad is a minister, and at times we would have church services at home. I still remember when I was about 12, he preached, "God is not a man in the sky. He is within you." That simple concept changed everything for me.

So, what does it mean to be a god with a small g? We are all within God and God is within us.

A splash of the ocean is still the ocean. A leaf from the tree still holds its wisdom. A spark of God is god. You have the power to transform your life from the inside out. You create your masterpiece, moment by moment, day by day.

In this divine dance of creation, where we recognize ourselves as gods with a small 'g', emerges the role of the superconscious. This is like a direct line to the wisdom and power of the Divine. It's the highest form of consciousness, where your individual self merges with your cosmic self. The superconscious is about tapping into a deeper, universal source.

When you connect with your superconscious, you align with the same force that shapes stars and spins galaxies. It's where your personal intentions meet universal truths. In this sacred space, we don't just manifest our desires; we co-create with the Divine. This empowers us to bring forth not just what we think we want, but what aligns with the greater good.

Embracing the superconscious means seeing beyond the ordinary, reaching into a realm where juicy miracles are everyday occurrences. It's recognizing that the divine force active within you is not separate from the infinite. By tapping into this higher consciousness, you unlock your true potential to create, to transform, and to live as you were born to be.

At the end of the last century, I headed to Los Angeles as a recent college grad to make it as an actress and writer. After being told I was too dark, too fat, and even too smart, I came back home, heartbroken, and disillusioned. I wanted to perform, write, make movies, and teach empowerment.

I put together my writings for a hip-hop "choreopoem," borrowing the term from Ntozake Shange. I had met her a few years earlier and remained obsessed with her work. I had been a teen rapper and hip-hop was my poetic love. I collaborated with my friend Antoy Grant on a three-woman show that became "Goddess City," now acknowledged as the world's very first hip-hop theater stage play.[21]

The premise of the show is that three goddesses come to save the Earth but forget that they are goddesses. They must live the painful experiences of earthly women to remember their truth.

Sound familiar?

When people ask why we were so successful, I often say that as twentysomething women, we didn't understand that we were not supposed to be. We proceeded as if we were the operant power and found ourselves supported by luminaries from August Wilson and Ruby Dee to Amiri and Amina Baraka.

Lots of folks thought we were blaspheming by calling ourselves goddesses and yelled at us in many ways, "Who do you think you are?"

Our answer? Goddesses.

At one event a famous woman poet we idolized mocked us on stage. It was humiliating. People had a hard time accepting that spiritual empowerment message from us. They didn't think we looked like we had the gravitas to discuss the topics we were discussing. Meanwhile, the show was about remembering who we all really are.

Neville said that he's glad that he didn't judge Abdullah as a potential spiritual guide based on appearances.

Abdullah once asked Neville to teach a class in Hebrew while he was a novice who didn't know a word of the language. This naturally really pissed off a classmate who was a Hebrew teacher. He could not understand why Abdullah chose Neville, a complete beginner, to teach. He had only been there a few months and Abdullah invited him to the blackboard.

Abdullah admonished the student with, "You do not know who he is. Neither does he remember who he is. If you only knew who he was you would sit right now at his feet. But you don't know who he is. Neither does he remember who he is."[22]

Six months later, Neville was indeed instructing the very same Hebrew teacher. He unlocked knowledge that he didn't know he had.

Each of us has a unique role to play in the world. And here I am decades later teaching the same gospel. You think that this is a book about manifesting. That is a start, but it is really a book about waking up and remembering who you really are.

You are the operant power.

How to Harness This Law: Your Imagination

He is in you as your own wonderful I Am ness.

— NEVILLE

It all comes back to Abdullah's key teaching: Your imagination is God. Let's dive a little deeper into this, shall we?

Neville's friend, writer Israel Regardie, says that Abdullah taught Neville that, "God and man being entirely one . . . The core of man's being was God—even though man in his blindness and ignorance did not know it. Outside of man there was nothing that man had not himself created. The entire world was a picture world, projected from within."[23]

Think of your imagination as the divine spark within you, or as the god, with a small g, that lives within you. It's through your imagination that you give life to your thoughts, your dreams, your hopes, and your desires. And as the god of your life, you can choose what to bring into your reality through this incredible power.

When you align your imagination with your deepest truths, you become an active participant in your life, creating your own reality instead of just passively witnessing it.

So, don't fear this power. Embrace it. Revel in it. It is your birthright, a gift from the Divine, and an integral part of who you are. You are not in the universe; the universe is in you.

Is This Blasphemy?

I get it. The idea that "we are gods, small g" might have hit a nerve, stirring up feelings of unease, or even fear. You might be thinking, "Isn't it arrogant or sacrilegious to even consider such a concept?"

Take a deep breath. Let's sit with this together for a moment.

When we say, "we are gods, small g," we are not implying that we're replacing or challenging God, the Grand Divine, the Higher Power, the Universe, or however define that greater consciousness.

We are just acknowledging the divinity that resides within each of us. This idea is threaded through ancient spiritual traditions globally. For those with a Christian background, when Jesus says, "I have said you are gods," he is pointing toward the divine spark within you. This spark, or the "operant power" as Neville referred to it, is the piece of God, the piece of the Infinite, that resides within all beings. In Hinduism, there's a belief in the "Atman," or the individual soul, which is part of the universal soul or "Brahman." In the Yoruba tradition, the concept of "Ori" represents our innermost spiritual self that is the divine within us.

We're talking about recognizing that piece of the Universal Consciousness, the Great Spirit, God, that resides in every being. We're talking about honoring our innate ability to create change in our lives, to manifest our dreams, to heal and grow and evolve.

This isn't about ego or arrogance. It's about empowerment and responsibility. It's about stepping into our roles as co-creators in our lives.

So, beautiful, if this concept has stirred up discomfort within you, I invite you to sit with it. Mull it over. Ask questions. Challenge it.

Whether you choose to see yourself as a god, small g, or in any other way, what matters is that it empowers you, brings you peace, and helps you live a life that's aligned with your heart's deepest calling.

You are the operant power in your life.

Exercise: Reverend Ike's Affirmative Treatment

Purpose: To activate your divine essence, beginning with Reverend Ike's statement:

"The truth of me is health.
God-in-me is my health!

The truth of me is happiness.
I am such a happy person that everybody likes to be around me.

The truth of me is love.
I AM surrounded by love.

The truth of me is success and prosperity.
God-in-me gives me new and exciting ideas that make me successful and prosperous.

The truth of me is money.
The money-making Mind of God-in-me gives me right ideas that bring money and great things into my life.
Thank you God-in-me!" [23]

What to do:

1. **Find a peaceful space.** This is sacred time for your personal empowerment.
2. **Relax.** Take deep breaths with your eyes closed to quiet your body and mind, readying yourself to harness your operant power.
3. **Focus.** Read the first line of the affirmative statement, "The truth of me is health," and recognize that you have the operant power to make it true for you.
4. **Personalize and affirm.** Close your eyes and say, "God-in-me is my health!" Feel this truth resonate within you as you claim your role as the operant power in your own life.
5. **Visualize.** Imagine the light of radiant health filling every cell in your body. Feel the energy of your already manifested desire.
6. **Continue.** Move on to the next affirmation, repeating steps 3 to 5.
7. **Complete the set.** Work through each affirmation slowly, feeling the weight and power of each statement, asserting yourself as the operant power each time.
8. **Seal the process.** Once you've finished, acknowledge the Divine within by saying three times, "Thank you, God-in-me!" This seals the process and cements your role as the operant power in your life.
9. **Create a daily ritual.** Engage with these affirmations every day. Choose either the morning to set a positive tone for the day, or the evening to let the affirmations manifest as you sleep.

10. **Reflect and adapt.** After a week, think about any shifts in your mindset or life circumstances. Notice how you are becoming more aware of your operant power. Adjust the affirmations if you feel the need.

Exercise: Reverend Ike's "The Theater of the Mind" for Spiritual Manifestation

Purpose: To unlock the potential of your "inner eye of faith" to manifest joy and prosperity, as Neville put it, "far beyond your wildest dreams."

According to *The New York Times,* "During the collection, [Reverend Ike] often leads the meeting into what he calls 'The Theater of the Mind,' a ritual that transports advocates into a 'closing of the two outer eyes, the opening of the inner eye of faith,' and enables them to visualize, then realize, states of contentment and prosperity ('I'm on that cruise to the islands, my bills are paid, I have money, I'm eating the steaks I enjoy, I am led into success and the prosperity to make all this possible because my Lord in me, the law of mind, guides me there . . .')."

What to do:

1. **Prepare the space.** Find a quiet and peaceful space where you won't be disturbed. This is your time to manifest your innermost desires.
2. **Calm the mind.** Take deep, calming breaths to steady your mind. Close your physical eyes, preparing to open your inner "eye of faith."

3. **Open the inner eye.** Imagine that your two physical eyes are closed but a third eye, your inner eye of faith, is opening in the middle of your forehead.

4. **See beyond seeing.** Visualize what happiness and prosperity look like for you. Is it a debt-free life, a romantic getaway, or perhaps a successful creative venture? Be as vivid and detailed as you can.

5. **Narrate your visualization.** Speak your vision out loud, just like Rev. Ike did. For example, say, "I'm on that cruise to the islands, my bills are paid, I have money . . ."

6. **Invoke your operant power.** As you list your desires, acknowledge that these manifestations are possible because of the "God-in-you." Say something like, "All things are possible due to the God-in-Me!"

7. **Soak it in.** Pause and dwell in this mental state for a few minutes, absorbing the feelings of happiness and prosperity.

8. **Seal the vision.** Close the session by saying, "Thank you, God-in-me!" This locks in your vision and affirms your role as the operant power.

Your Operant Power Decree

I make my life happen. There is no other person in charge of me. Today, and every day hereafter, I stand strong in the belief that I am the power in my life. The strength of my spirit and of my mind guide me.

I am the power in my life.

No longer will I surrender my will to the random events and circumstances of the world. Instead, I will shape these events and circumstances with the chisel of my intention, carving out a reality that resonates with my desires.

My destiny is not written in the stars, but in my heart, my mind, and in the strength of my spirit. Every day, with every breath, I affirm this truth: I am the power in my life. And as the sun sets on each day, I will rest in the knowledge that I have used this power wisely.

And so it is.

Your Operant Power Journal Questions

- How does knowing you're the operant power change the way you see past challenges?
- How can you use this insight to tackle future hurdles differently?
- What kinds of thoughts, feelings, and beliefs would align your inner world with your dream reality?

THE MYSTERY OF EVERYONE IS YOU PUSHED OUT

The creatures are not judged or condemned for the seeming wrongs they do, for the Lord himself ordained all deeds.

— NEVILLE[24]

Relationships are at the heart of our human experience. They are the threads that connect us. We may choose to label our relationships as familial, romantic, friendly, or professional, but at the core of each connection is the truth that we depend on one another.

It's easy to feel spiritually elevated when we're alone, meditating on a "mountaintop," removed from the everyday frustrations and triggers. In solitude, it's easier to control our thoughts and emotions. As Louise Hay used to say, it's easy to feel good in a seminar, but then in the parking lot you're cursing at the person who cut you off!

The real test of our self-mastery is in our interactions with each other. That's when our unresolved wounds, triggers, and and reactive patterns come to the surface, giving us the opportunity to grow.

So, how would you feel if I told you that everyone is you? The cheating ex, the faithful bestie, the dubious doctor? What if each person who cut you off in traffic is a reflection of your inner world, revealing aspects of yourself that you may not have been aware of? The principle of "Everyone Is You Pushed Out" (EIYPO) says that the external world, including the people in it, mirrors our internal beliefs and assumptions. This can be both freeing and overwhelming. You have the power to shape your relationships but also the responsibility to address the parts of yourself that you avoid.

In 1930 or '31, Abdullah "the grand old man" gave Neville a written Kabbalah teaching with the reminder, "Creatures are never guilty of the seeming wrongs they do. The Lord ordained all deeds, and he alone performs all that is performed."[25] Abdullah is teaching that the actions of those around us, and indeed all events in life, are not random or isolated. Instead, they're part of a greater design, crafted by our Higher Power, Universal God Consciousness. This divine power, orchestrating every action and reaction, is intricately linked to our own inner state. Abdullah's insight implies that what we perceive and experience is closely tied to what's happening within us—our thoughts, beliefs, and innermost feelings. This sets the stage for 'Everyone Is You Pushed Out,' where we recognize the world around us as a reflection of our internal world. It's a deep concept, but when combined with the idea of EIYPO, or "Everyone Is You Pushed Out," it starts making a lot of sense.

Imagine for a moment that everyone around you acts as a mirror, reflecting parts of your own consciousness—both the good and the challenges. For instance, if someone upsets you, they might be echoing a belief or insecurity you hold about yourself or the world. This isn't about self-blame but about recognizing the power of your beliefs in shaping your interactions.

As Louise Hay said, "Everyone is a reflection of us, and what we see in another person we can see in ourselves."[26]

With this perspective, we can transform the way we approach relationships. Instead of wondering, "Why did they do that?" we can ask ourselves, "What inside of me expected or resonated with that behavior?" By understanding and changing our inner beliefs, we get to transform the reflection we see in others.

It's an empowering way to navigate life. Every relationship offers a clue, a lesson about our own beliefs and feelings. When we embrace this, we don't just experience relationships; we evolve through them.

EIYPO can be fun to experiment with too. As I write this, it's August in New York City and I am on the porch of my new home. I have been ranting about how quiet the neighborhood has gotten and how much life it had back in the day. Lo and behold, today one of my neighbors now has a loud-talking visitor blasting louder music from his car in the middle of the workday. I am super annoyed. So I tried an experiment to make him go away. I focused on how quiet the block is.

I was tempted to sing along to some of his car radio's old-school hits, but I am on deadline to get these teachings to you. So I ignored the evidence to the contrary (Tupac rapping "Dear Mama") and focused on being grateful for how quiet the block is, and how wonderful it is that I can focus on my work. I ignored how settled-in the friend seemed—and sure enough—he just suddenly realized he had somewhere else to be.

Phew! Everyone is you pushed out.

The idea of EIYPO is the belief that our outer world, including our relationships, is a direct reflection of our inner world. Our thoughts, feelings, and beliefs about ourselves, others, and the world shape the experiences we have and the people we have in our lives. Life is a gigantic mirror, reflecting back to us our own consciousness. The people we interact with are like mirrors, reflecting aspects of our own inner state. In other words, they are us, pushed out.

This means that the people you encounter and experience are largely influenced by your inner beliefs and feelings about relationships, love, trust, communication, and so on. The way people treat you, the conversations you have, the love you receive or don't receive—all of these are reflections of your own inner world. When you change your inner beliefs and feelings, you change the reflection in the mirror—and you change your relationships.

Now, let's be clear. Embracing the concept of EIYPO does not mean that you're solely responsible for every potential jerk you encounter. Life is complex, and other people have their own free will, beliefs, and emotions that contribute to the dynamics. What EIYPO does mean is that you have tremendous power to shape and influence your relationships by shifting your internal state.

The Relationship Mirror

Have you ever experienced "same dude, different pants"? Sometimes we find ourselves caught in recurring patterns and relationship dramas. Been there, done that. If you find yourself experiencing the same dynamics over and over again, regardless of the person involved, it's time to wake up to the fact that the common denominator is you. This isn't meant to blame or shame you, but to empower you to change the patterns you see. Your relationships are mirrors reflecting your innermost beliefs, expectations, and feelings back to you.

Each person you interact with reflects a part of your consciousness, like fragments of a mirror showing you aspects of your inner self. When we talk about recurring patterns in relationships, we're talking about recurring reflections of your internal state. These patterns offer powerful insights into your beliefs, expectations, and feelings.

The challenge is that recognizing these patterns isn't always easy. We're often so immersed in our dramas that we don't immediately see the reflections.

Recognize your patterns. Begin by observing your relationships and interactions. Pay attention to how you feel, how you react, and the dynamics. Do you often feel unheard or disrespected? Do you feel loved and valued? What commonalities do you notice across different relationships?

Exercise: Exploring Your Relationship Patterns

Purpose: To see how the beliefs you hold about yourself are reflected in the behavior and actions of those around you.

Are your interactions filled with understanding and respect? Or do you find yourself often mired in conflict? These external experiences are direct reflections of your internal landscape.

What to do:

Reflect on your beliefs and expectations. What ideas or expectations do you have about yourself, others, or relationships in general? Can you think of where these might come from? Maybe they're linked to past experiences, things you were told growing up, or even messages from the media. How do these beliefs show up in the way you act, talk, and make choices in your relationships?

Observe your emotions. Pay attention to the emotions that often come up when you're with others. What feelings keep popping up? Think about what these emotions might be telling you about your inner world.

By reflecting on these questions, you can start to uncover how your inner beliefs and emotions are influencing your relationships. This insight is a powerful step toward transforming these patterns and creating more fulfilling connections. Remember, understanding yourself is the first step in understanding your relationships.

Approach this exploration with compassion for yourself. Recognizing patterns can bring up feelings of guilt or shame, but know that these emotions are natural and part of the healing process.

Guilt can be a sign that you're ready to make amends and take different actions. Shame, however, can be more insidious. If you feel that you're fundamentally flawed or unworthy, you have to address this belief. Shame can stem from past traumas, negative messages you received about yourself, or experiences where you felt rejected or unlovable.

Healing shame requires self-compassion, self-acceptance, and often support from trusted friends, family, or counselors. As you start to release shame and embrace your worthiness, you'll naturally shift your internal state, and your relationships will begin to reflect this transformation.

Question your beliefs. Are they true? Are they serving you? If not, replace them with beliefs that support your well-being and the relationships you desire. If you've believed that you're unworthy of love, replace that belief with the truth that you deserve love and respect.

As you change your inner world, you'll start to see different reflections in your relationship mirror. New dynamics will unfold, and different people will be attracted into your life.

The Power of Self-Love

The way we treat ourselves sets the tone for how others treat us. The love and acceptance we show ourselves get mirrored back to us in our interactions with others. Self-love isn't a catchphrase. It's a potent, active force that shapes your life and relationships.

As we touched on in the Mystery of Vibration, when you love and accept yourself unconditionally, you give off a frequency of self-assuredness and self-acceptance. When you approach relationships from a place of self-love, you're not looking for someone else to complete you or validate you. You're already whole, and you're looking for those who resonate with that wholeness.

By cultivating self-love, you naturally create relationships that match your frequency of self-acceptance. You manifest partners who recognize your worth because you see it in yourself. You attract and create interactions that are respectful and loving because that's how you treat yourself.

Self-love involves making choices that prioritize your well-being, setting boundaries, speaking kindly to yourself, and forgiving yourself. As you embody these actions, you create space for more harmonious interactions.

Imagine entering a relationship not from a place of neediness or lack but from a place of abundance and wholeness. This shift doesn't just change the dynamics of your relationships; it changes the people you attract. You start vibing with folks who also operate from a place of self-love, and together, you create interactions that are balanced, respectful, and harmonious.

How Neville Manifested His Specific Person in a Week

At 18 years old, Neville got married, had a son, and then he and his wife separated that same year. They never got a divorce, so technically, they were still married. Fast forward 16 years. Neville falls head over heels in love with another woman. He's sure that she's the one he wants to marry. But there's a problem: he's still legally married to his first wife.

So what does Neville do? He decides to use the Law to shift things. After all, everyone is you pushed out, right?

Every night, he lays down in his hotel room and closes his eyes. Instead of imagining the empty room he's in, he visualizes an apartment where he and his new love are living together. He sees her in one bed and himself in another (that's how successful married couples of the time slept). He feels the joy, the love, and the warmth of being with her. He does this night after night, fully feeling as if it's already true.

Even though there are people, like his dancing partner, who try to keep him and his new love apart, Neville doesn't give up. He keeps living in his imagined reality, seeing it from the end, feeling the love and happiness he wants.

Then, out of the blue, Neville gets a call. He has to go to court, but he doesn't know why. He thinks it's probably a prank, so he ignores it. But then he gets another call, this time telling him that his estranged wife is on trial for shoplifting.

His first wife was caught stealing from a store. Neville could have used this to get his divorce, but he stands up in court and passionately defends her. The judge is moved by his words and suspends her sentence. Feeling immense gratitude, his wife agrees to sign the divorce papers.

The thing is, his wife had no reason to be in New York City. But she ended up there, and her actions led to Neville getting the divorce he wanted. He didn't ask for it; he didn't force it. It just happened.

Instead of trying to force things externally, Neville turned inward. He visualized a reality where he was already living happily with his new love, embodying the feelings and emotions associated with that desired outcome. Neville's inner state and beliefs were reflected back to him through the actions of his estranged wife.

Neville didn't have to persuade or manipulate her. The people around him were simply mirroring the new reality he had created within himself.

He explained it:

> All you need to know is what you want. Construct a scene which would imply the fulfillment of your desire. Enter the scene and remain there. If your imaginal counselor (your feeling of fulfillment) agrees with that which is used to illustrate your fulfilled desire, your fantasy will become a fact. If it does not, start all over again by creating a new scene and enter it.[27]

Exercise: Transform Existing Relationships Using EIYPO

Purpose: To identify and shift beliefs and patterns that affect your relationships whether that be with family, friends, business associates, or romantic partners.

What to do:

1. **Identify your current beliefs and patterns.** Take note of recurring themes, reactions, and patterns in your relationships. What beliefs about yourself and others are being reflected? Do you often feel unappreciated, undervalued, or misunderstood? Recognize the patterns and ask yourself what assumptions you hold that could be contributing to these experiences.

2. **Replace blocked beliefs with empowering ones.** If you find that certain beliefs or assumptions negatively affecting your relationships, replace them with more empowering ones. For example, if you believe that people always take advantage of you, shift that belief to "I am respected and valued by the people around me."

3. **Feel your desired reality.** Spend time in meditation or quiet reflection and immerse yourself in the feelings of already having the transformed relationships you desire. Feel the love, respect, and understanding as if they were already a reality.

4. **Visualize new interactions.** Create mental images that reflect your new beliefs and assumptions. Imagine specific scenarios in which you and the other person are interacting in ways that align with what you really want.

5. **Revise past events.** Use The Revision Process (see Bonus Processes at the end) to mentally revisit and change past interactions that were unsatisfactory or hurtful. Imagine the events unfolding differently, in ways that align with your new beliefs and desired outcomes.

6. **Affirm your new beliefs.** Use affirmations to reinforce your new beliefs and assumptions about your relationships. For example, "I am loved, respected, and understood by my family."

7. **Practice gratitude.** Focus on the positive aspects of your relationships and express gratitude for them.

8. **Communicate openly.** While working on your internal state is crucial, it's also essential to have open and honest conversations with the people involved in your relationships. Share your feelings, needs, and desires in a respectful and clear manner.

9. **Let go and trust the process.** After doing the inner work, let go of the need to control or force the outcome. Trust that as you shift your internal state, the external reflection in your relationships will naturally improve.

10. **Celebrate positive changes.** Acknowledge and celebrate any improvements or positive changes in your relationships, no matter how small. Recognize that these changes are a reflection of your transformed beliefs and assumptions.

Exercise: Manifest Your Ideal Relationships

Purpose: To create your ideal relationships, beyond just manifesting a specific person (SP) using the power of visualization, combined with the EIYPO principle.

What to do:

1. **Understand your desires**. Begin by understanding what you desire in relationships, beyond just an SP. What qualities and dynamics do you want to experience in your relationships with friends, family, colleagues, or others?

2. **Define your ideal relationships.** Clearly define what your ideal relationships look like. How do you interact with others? What do conversations feel like? What kind of shared experiences do you have? Define the boundaries, mutual respect, and understanding present in these relationships.

3. **Engage your subconscious mind.** Your subconscious mind is a powerful tool for manifesting your desires. It absorbs and internalizes your beliefs, making them a part of your core identity. By feeding it positive and empowering beliefs about relationships, you set the stage for your subconscious to work toward manifesting these beliefs in your reality.

4. **Visualize.** Regularly imagine yourself in scenarios where you are experiencing your ideal relationships. Feel the emotions, hear the conversations, and see the interactions in your mind's eye. Engage all your senses in this visualization. The more real it feels, the more effectively it will influence your subconscious mind.

5. **Align.** Be sure that your thoughts and feelings are aligned with the relationships you are trying to manifest. Avoid negativity, doubt, or blocked beliefs. Instead, cultivate feelings of love, respect, and appreciation for others, as well as for yourself.

6. **Use affirmations.** Affirmations like "I am worthy of love and respect," "My relationships are harmonious and fulfilling," or "I easily connect with others" can help reprogram your subconscious mind to align with your relationship goals.

7. **Act "as if."** Behave as if your ideal relationships are already a reality. Treat others with the respect, understanding, and kindness that you want to be treated with. Are you as loving, compassionate, and generous as you expect others to be?

8. **Understand creating vs. attracting.** Manifesting your ideal relationships is more about creating than attracting. You are not passively waiting for the right people to come into your life. Instead, you are actively shaping your inner world to create the outer world you desire.

9. **Let go of resistance.** Let go of any resistance or preconceived notions about how and when you will manifest. Trust the process and allow the Divine to work its magic.

10. **Practice gratitude.** Practice gratitude for the relationships you currently have, even if they are not yet ideal.

EIYPO and Structural Injustices: Understanding the Balance

As we discussed earlier, one criticism often leveled against manifestation processes like "Everyone Is You Pushed Out" is that they can, unintentionally, seem to place blame on victims of structural injustices such as racism, sexism, homophobia, and crimes like abuse, trafficking, and police brutality. It's a valid concern.

First of all, I can't stress this enough: no one is responsible for the prejudice, discrimination, or violence inflicted upon them due to their race, gender, sexual orientation, or any other identity marker. These are societal, systemic issues, not individual failures or manifestations. People who face such injustices are not "attracting" them or creating these experiences due to negative thinking or incorrect manifestation.

However, in saying this, we don't negate the personal power and potential for transformation that universal laws like EIYPO can offer us within these structural realities.

Here's how you can use EIYPO without falling into the trap of victim-blaming:

- **Acknowledge structural realities.** Recognize that we live within societal structures that have their own dynamics. These structures can significantly influence our experiences, and acknowledging this is the first step toward meaningful change.
- **Embrace your personal power.** While systemic issues exist, don't lose sight of your personal power. You have the ability to shape your attitudes, beliefs, and responses.

- **Use EIYPO as a tool for empowerment.** Use the concept of EIYPO to foster a mindset of empowerment. Manifest positive change in your personal life, relationships, and immediate surroundings. Work toward creating a safe, supportive, and empowering environment for yourself and others.
- **Advocate for change.** Use your power to advocate for structural change. Stand up against injustices, use your voice, and work collectively with others. Your personal empowerment can fuel your drive for wider societal change.

Your EIYPO Decree

I am the architect of my relationships. Every interaction I have, every connection I experience, is a mirror of my own thoughts, beliefs, and emotions.

Today I choose to lay a foundation of love, respect, and kindness within myself. As I fill my inner being with these qualities, I see them mirrored back to me. I consciously and intentionally select beliefs that foster joyful, fulfilling, and loving connections.

I am deserving of relationships that bring joy, love, and mutual respect. I am the architect of my relationships, and I affirm this truth every day, watching as it is reflected back to me in my world. I no longer passively accept what life brings my way.

I am the architect of my relationships. As I nurture myself, and as I honor my needs and my boundaries, I set the stage for others to do the same.

Your EIYPO Journal Questions

- Are there any patterns in your relationships? Could these patterns be linked to how you view yourself or others?
- How do you want to feel in your dream relationships?
- When you have a disagreement, how can you use the idea that "everyone is you pushed out" to better understand? What could these situations be telling you about what you need or what you haven't yet healed within yourself?

THE MYSTERY OF IDENTICAL HARVEST

But you know that God made everything? Everything is God. You would assume that he made some things and not the rest? No, God made everything.

— Abdullah

The Law of Identical Harvest is grounded in the idea that we reap what we sow. In other words, the circumstances of our lives are a direct reflection of the thoughts, beliefs, and feelings that we have planted within our consciousness. By understanding this principle, we can become more deliberate creators of our own reality.

Neville explains this law as a fundamental principle that governs the universe, and it's grounded in the biblical teaching that "what you sow, so shall you reap."

This law is a reminder of the responsibility we have in shaping our own reality. If you don't know by now, your imagination is a powerful tool for creating your desired outcome, and you must be mindful of the seeds you sow. It's time to take control of your thoughts and imaginal acts, planting seeds that align with your desired outcome, to manifest the life of your dreams.

Neville said, Abdullah, "taught me scripture as I never heard it from my mother's knee or from my minister or from anyone who taught me the Bible before. It became a book that was alive to me under the guidance of Abdullah."[28]

He said that Abdullah "was a Black man, raised in the Jewish faith, but really understood Christianity as few men that I ever met understood it."[29]

Abdullah, as a Jewish rabbi who taught about Jesus, clearly transcended religious doctrine boundaries. His teachings focused on universal truths that underpin all spiritual traditions. Abdullah emphasized the transformative power of belief and the conscious use of imagination to manifest desires. He bridged the gap between the traditional narratives of Judaism and Christianity, shedding light on Jesus Christ as a symbol of spiritual awakening, love, and unity.

Abdullah's teachings centered on the Law of Identical Harvest, known as the Law of Cause and Effect in New Thought philosophy. This principle states that what we sow in our imagination and beliefs, we reap in our external reality. Abdullah saw this universal law embedded in the teachings of Jesus Christ but also in the wisdom of many other spiritual traditions.

As we discussed in the Abdullah Paradigm, one of the cornerstones of Abdullah's teachings was the importance of understanding and really internalizing John 17, known as the "High Priestly Prayer." In this chapter, Jesus, as the high priest after the order of Melchizedek, prays for the unity and sanctification of his disciples and all future believers. He speaks of the oneness he shares with the Father and the love that exists between them.

Abdullah recognized the profound message of unity, love, and spiritual awakening in this prayer. He saw it as an expression of the interconnectedness of all beings with the source of creation and an embodiment of the principles underpinning the Law of Identical Harvest. Abdullah encouraged his students to commit this chapter to memory. He believed that by understanding and internalizing this prayer, they could cultivate a deeper sense of oneness with the Divine and harness the power of intention and belief to manifest their deepest desires.

In Abdullah's gatherings, as described by Neville, students would rise at the end of the meeting and recite the 17th chapter of John together. Abdullah would close with the words, "Praise be unto that unity that is our unity, one in all and all in one." This ritual is the essence of the Law of Identical Harvest—the idea that what we sow in our hearts, we reap in our reality.

By embracing the message of unity and love in this prayer, we align ourselves with the spiritual principles underlying the Law of Identical Harvest. As we sow seeds of love, unity, and intention within our consciousness, we create a fertile ground for a harvest reflecting our true nature and desires. Abdullah's teachings serve as a reminder that the truth of manifesting is not confined to any single religious tradition or dogma. It is a universal principle found in the teachings of Jesus and the wisdom of many other global spiritual traditions. By focusing on the underlying truth and applying it in our lives, we can transcend rigid, separatist limitations and experience the transformative power of spiritual insight and manifesting through the Law of Identical Harvest.

Here is what Neville had to say about it:

> I can't conceive of anything more beautiful than that 17th of John. When you read it and you get lost in it, I defy you to just restrain the tears. It's the one chapter that old Ab, my friend Abdullah, insisted that we commit to memory. Everyone had to know it. No reading of books. . . . And then he

> would close always with "Praise be unto that unity that is our unity, one in all and all in one." We all had to simply rise at the close of the meeting and recite the 17th of John. It was driven into the mind of everyone who was present. You read it, if you do not know it, you read it when you go home.[30]

The Origin of the Law of Identical Harvest

The Law of Identical Harvest is deeply rooted in biblical teachings. In Genesis 1:24, God commands the earth to bring forth vegetation and fruit-bearing trees, each "according to its kind," highlighting the idea that the seeds we plant will yield a harvest that is identical to the type of seed sown. In Galatians 6:7, we are reminded that we will reap what we sow, and that the laws of the universe are in perfect order.

Take it from Neville:

> "The law of identical harvest or cause and effect is impersonal and can be used to bring into your experience anything you can conceive. Since creation is finished, every possible state already exists. Your fusion with a particular state (imagining with feeling what you would experience were you in that state) causes that state to be projected on your screen of space. This law cannot be changed or broken and always reproduces in your outer world the exact duplicate of any belief you consent to as true. If you would change your world, you must change your beliefs. Since consciousness is the only cause, you cannot blame others for the conditions which presently exist, nor can fate or chance be the cause of that which you are now experiencing. Nothing can alter the course of events in your life except a change in your own consciousness."

The Law of Identical Harvest is intrinsically connected to the principles of cause and effect, as well as the idea of sowing and reaping. Every thought, belief, or feeling that we entertain becomes a cause that sets in motion a series of effects that eventually manifest in our physical reality. Just as a farmer sows seeds and expects to harvest crops that are identical to the seeds planted, so too do we harvest the results of the mental seeds we have sown.

This law operates impersonally and automatically, reproducing in our external world the exact duplicate of our internal beliefs. It underscores the importance of being mindful of the thoughts and beliefs we entertain, as they are the seeds that will determine the nature of our harvest. By consciously choosing positive and empowering beliefs, we can plant the seeds for a life that reflects our deepest desires.

Understanding the Cause and Effect Cycle

The Law of Identical Harvest is a fundamental principle that governs the unfolding of events. At the core of this law is the understanding that every cause has an effect, and every effect has a cause. In the context of manifestation, our thoughts, beliefs, and imaginal acts serve as causes that produce effects in the form of the circumstances and events of our lives.

Our thoughts and beliefs shape our perceptions, attitudes, and emotions. They form the paradigm or mental framework we use to interpret and respond to the world around us. Every thought we entertain and every belief we hold sends out a vibrational frequency that interacts with the energy of the universe. As a result, we create experiences that are in resonance with the frequency of our thoughts and beliefs. This is the essence of the Law of Life.

Our beliefs, in particular, play a pivotal role in shaping our reality. As Neville teaches, our assumptions about ourselves and the world form the foundation upon which our experiences are built. When we hold positive, empowering beliefs, we create a fertile ground for the manifestation of our desires. On the other hand, when we entertain blocked beliefs, we restrict the flow of abundance and hinder the realization of our dreams.

Examples of Cause and Effect

The law of cause and effect operates in every area of our lives, from our relationships and finances to our health and well-being.

Here are a few examples from my Goddess Womanifesting Community:

- **Relationships:** "Harmony" harbors feelings of unworthiness and believes she is unlovable. These beliefs serve as causes that produce effects in the form of unsatisfying relationships, rejection, or loneliness. On the other hand, "Kenya," who cultivates self-love and believes she is deserving of healthy, loving relationships creates partnerships that reflect and affirm those beliefs.
- **Finances:** "Tonia" constantly worries about money and imagines scenarios of lack and struggle is planting seeds of financial hardship. As a result, she experiences cycles of financial challenges and setbacks. On the other hand, "Didi," who holds beliefs of abundance and imagines themselves enjoying financial prosperity is more likely to create opportunities for wealth and success.

- **Health:** Our thoughts and beliefs about our health play a significant role in our physical well-being. A person who constantly imagines themselves falling ill or believes they are prone to sickness may manifest those very conditions in their body. On the other hand, a person who affirms their health and imagines themselves as strong and vibrant is more likely to enjoy robust physical health.

The Law of Identical Harvest teaches us that we reap what we sow, both in our thoughts and in our actions. By understanding the cause and effect cycle, we can consciously plant seeds, paving the way for a life filled with abundant love, joy, health and riches.

Exercise: Manifest with the Law of Identical Harvest

Purpose: To become a conscious creator of your own life experience.

What to do:

1. **Identify your desires.** The first step in manifesting with the Law of Identical Harvest is to get clear on what you desire. Consider what you want to experience in your life, whether it's a fulfilling relationship, a successful career, or vibrant health. Write down your desires in detail, and be as specific as you can.

2. **Sow the right seeds.** In order to reap a specific harvest, you must first plant the appropriate seeds. In the context of manifestation, the seeds you plant are your thoughts, beliefs, and

emotions. Begin by replacing any blocked beliefs or negative thoughts with positive and empowering beliefs. Visualize your desires as already fulfilled and cultivate the corresponding emotions, such as joy, gratitude, and excitement.

3. **Cultivate the right conditions.** Just as plants need the right conditions to grow, so do the seeds of your desires. This involves maintaining a positive mental and emotional environment, as well as taking inspired action that aligns with your goals. Avoid negativity, practice gratitude, and stay focused on your desired outcome.

4. **Take inspired action.** Every manifestation is different, but don't pooh-pooh action. Here's what Neville had to say about it: "First of all, a thought unless it moves man into action is not creative. A thought by itself does nothing, doesn't affect anything. So how do I take a thought and sow it that I can really make it become effective and it moves through this series from a thought, to an act, to a habit, to a character, to a destiny?"[30]

5. **Use the power of imagination.** Use your imagination to vividly visualize your desires as already realized. Immerse yourself in the experience, engaging all your senses, and feel the emotions associated with your desire.

6. **Let go and trust.** Once you have planted the seeds of your desire, let go of the outcome and trust that the Law of Identical Harvest will work in your favor. Avoid obsessing over the details or trying to force the manifestation. Instead, trust that life will bring about the right conditions for your harvest at the right time.

7. **Embrace revision.** If you encounter

circumstances that don't align with your desires, you can use The Revision Process (in the Bonus section at the end) to change the outcome. In your imagination, revise the situation so that it unfolds according to your preferred outcome. This acts as a new seed that can overwrite the previous one.

8. **Recognize the harvest.** Keep an open heart and mind, and be on the lookout for signs that your harvest is manifesting. It may not always come in the form you expected, but it will always match the essence of the seeds you planted. When you recognize your harvest, express gratitude and appreciation.

9. **Understand the timing.** Just as a farmer understands that crops take time to grow, recognize that your manifestations may also require time to come to fruition. Be patient. Every seed has its own gestation period. Trust that your harvest will manifest at the perfect time for you.

How People Get Hindered with the Law of Identical Harvest

Understanding the Law of Identical Harvest is a powerful tool in the manifesting process, but many people find themselves tripped up by its principles.

There are several common pitfalls that can interfere with effectively using this law to manifest:

- **Lack of Awareness:** Many people go through life without understanding the connection between their thoughts, beliefs, and the circumstances of their lives. As a result, they unknowingly plant seeds that lead to undesired outcomes.

- **Negative Thought Patterns:** Another challenge people face is the habit of negative thinking. By continually focusing on what they don't want, they inadvertently plant seeds that lead to undesired outcomes. Break these patterns by shifting your focus to positive thoughts and desirable outcomes.
- **Impatience:** Some people become frustrated when their desires don't manifest immediately. They may give up on their goals, doubting the Law of Life. Every seed has its own gestation period, and manifestations may take time.
- **Inconsistency:** Some folks plant positive seeds but then water them with contradictory thoughts or actions. For example, they might visualize financial abundance but then reinforce scarcity by complaining about money.
- **Attachment to Outcomes:** Being too attached to a specific outcome can create resistance and hinder manifestation. Sometimes we become fixated on how and when our desires should manifest, which can block the natural flow of events. Let go and trust the process.
- **Lack of Self-belief:** Doubting your worthiness or ability to manifest can sabotage the process. When you don't believe you deserve your desires or question their ability to create your reality, you plant seeds of doubt that can prevent your desired outcomes.
- **Ignoring Inspired Action:** The Law of Identical Harvest also requires action. Some people may neglect to take inspired action that aligns with their goals, assuming that mere visualization is enough.
- **Overlooking the Harvest:** Sometimes, you may not recognize your harvest when it manifests.

The outcome may come in a different form than expected or may seem unrelated. Being open-minded and paying attention to the signs and synchronicities can help you recognize your manifested desires.

- **Neglecting Gratitude:** Failing to acknowledge and express gratitude for the manifestations can hinder future harvests. Gratitude amplifies the positive energy and helps create a more favorable environment for future seeds to grow.

Identical Harvest and Financial Prosperity: Sowing Seeds of Abundance

Your spiritual path is not separate from your financial path; they are intimately intertwined. How we do anything is how we do everything, right? Now is the time to step into your power and claim the financial abundance that is your birthright. It's not just possible; it's your divine right.

You are worthy and deserving of prosperity—don't let anyone tell you otherwise. You're not just meant to survive; you're designed to thrive.

The Law of Identical Harvest lights the path from scarcity to abundance and helps you navigate your money path. Just as you would plant seeds in fertile soil and expect a bountiful harvest, the thoughts and feelings you cultivate bear their own kind of fruit. By applying this law to money and prosperity, you activate a powerful force that can transform your financial life.

Each thought you have about money—whether it's a worry about bills, a dream of prosperity, or anything in between—has the power to shape your financial reality. These thoughts set into motion a chain of events and experiences that directly relate to what you believe about money.

It is my humble honor that I get to coach spiritual entrepreneurs. One of the biggest blocked beliefs I find holding back some of my most gifted Spiritpreneurs is the lie that money is not spiritual.

I've seen people argue that spiritual teachers, including those who draw upon the insights of Neville, Dr. Murphy, and Abdullah, should not charge for their work. They think charging for a book is okay, but charging for a session is a bad thing, but there is absolutely no difference.

They mistakenly think that Neville didn't charge for his wisdom. Neville's workshops were expensive. The reality is quite the opposite; Neville was not only open to the exchange of money for his teachings, but he also acknowledged money as a form of energy exchange. He was a great businessman.

My great-grandmother was a healer in Guyana, South America. She was supported by her community who paid in eggs, chickens, goats, and the like. That was the currency of the day. If you are a community healer today and get paid with cash, bitcoin, or plastic, there is no difference. That is the currency of your day. There is no difference from you telling me the cost of your services versus me paying what I think they are worth.

Abdullah charged Neville, but not in money, as Neville had none. We don't know how much the dignitaries paid for Abdullah's one-on-one time or the groups paid for his classes. Let's not dishonor him by assuming less. To believe that spiritual wisdom should be given away without remuneration is to devalue the time, energy, and expertise that go into sharing these teachings. This belief is a reflection of our own blocked beliefs about money. Neville paid in time and effort by cleaning for Abdullah, and time is arguably the most valuable currency there is. You can't get time back.

I would much rather pay for something with my money instead of paying with my time. You may feel differently and that's your right.

I invest lots of money in myself to be mentored, coached, and taught by incredible teachers. I also host international retreats and personal empowerment courses so I have lots of conversations around spirituality and money. A member of my community recently complained about the cost of a spiritual program, yet she was planning to travel first class to another country for front section seats at a sold-out Beyoncé concert. Great for her—I love Beyoncé. But it struck me how we determine value based on personal priorities. This just highlights that what we're willing to invest in reflects what we truly value. While some may expect teaching, coaching, and spiritual guidance to be free, others recognize and are willing to invest in their personal growth. It's a matter of individual choice and what each person deems valuable. You are not obligated to work with anyone. Someone could charge a million dollars for their services. It's up to them. It's up to us to say, this is for me or not for me. If others find value to pay it, great for them.

I had to make a huge shift in this area. I used to have big challenges around manifesting money, talking about money and charging for my intensive work—although I always give my all. I was terrified of being judged and I was burning out and suffering because of it. Now I love paying someone abundantly for their spiritual work and receiving abundant payment for my work as well. It feels good to have raised my earthly standards and treat myself with basic things like flying first class. I want my daughter to have comfort with abundance, so I had to make these changes within myself. It is impossible for me to "charge my worth" because I am valuable beyond measure, but I know that many people have had life-changing results working with me. I charge from the heart, sometimes that's free or a tiny number, sometimes it's a larger number, but it is always what feels in alignment with Divine energy.

If you believe that spiritual teachers should "charge a little, but not a lot," that is based on the flawed notion that there's a cap on spiritual or financial worth. This perspective implies that God consciousness somehow quantifies or limits abundance. But to the divine, it's all the same: limitless. Ten dollars for a book or $10,000 for one-on-one support is the same to the Divine. To think that one is superior to the other reflects our own fears of scarcity and lack.

By addressing and transforming these blocked beliefs, you open up the flow of abundance in your life. You align with the Law of Identical Harvest, planting seeds of prosperity that will bloom into a life of financial well-being.

Overcoming Your Financial Scarcity Mindset

You just got your paycheck, and before you even have a chance to feel that sweet relief, your mind starts racing through a list of all the bills, debts, and obligations waiting to gobble it up. It's like you're already financially "spoken for" before the money even hits your account. Or how about this—you avoid looking at your bank account because you're afraid of what you might find. You've convinced yourself that not knowing is better than facing a reality that might not be so pretty. Sound familiar?

You know you're deep in the scarcity mindset when you find yourself complaining or half-joking with your friends about "the high cost of gas or eggs" or "the struggles of being perpetually broke."

Hey, we've all been there, right?

When you operate from this scarcity mentality, you're sowing seeds of lack and limitation. According to the Law of Identical Harvest, you'll reap experiences that confirm this limiting view of your world. It's a self-fulfilling prophecy. You believe there won't be enough, so there never is. You're not just preserving the status quo; you're actively creating it. And the cycle continues—unless you choose to break it.

A scarcity mindset is like planting weeds in your garden of abundance. You're so focused on not having enough that you don't leave room energetically for more. And let's be real: if you're always thinking about what you lack, then according to the Law of Identical Harvest, you're just planting more seeds of "not enough."

So, how do you flip the script?

The Law of Identical Harvest isn't just woo-woo B.S.; it's a practical guide to life. What you focus on grows. So let's focus on abundance, prosperity, and all the things we desire. You in?

- **Recognize your blocked beliefs.** The first step in changing any mindset is to know it's there. Listen to your inner dialogue about money. If phrases like "Money is the root of all evil" or "You have to work hard to earn money" pop up, those are your weeds. Pluck 'em out!
- **Flip the script.** Once you've identified those scarcity thoughts, replace them with affirmations that serve you better. Instead of saying, "I never have enough money," try saying, "Money flows easily and abundantly to me."
- **Give to receive.** One of the fastest ways to shift from scarcity to abundance is to give. It can be money, time, or skills—whatever feels right. Giving signals to the universe that you have

plenty to share, which invites even more into your life.

- **Invest in yourself.** Sometimes spending money is the best way to make money, especially when you're investing in skills or tools that will pay off in the long run.
- **Celebrate small wins.** Every time you make a smart financial decision, give yourself a pat on the back. Positive reinforcement will help solidify your new, abundant mindset.
- **Visualize your abundance.** Close your eyes and imagine the life of financial abundance you desire. See it, smell it, and feel it. What does prosperity look like for you? A new home? A thriving business? Financial security for your family?
- **Write in a gratitude journal.** At the end of each day, jot down three things related to money and abundance that you're thankful for. It could be as simple as finding a coin on the street or as significant as landing a big client. What you appreciate, appreciates.

Exercise: Money Manifesting—Sowing Seeds of Abundance

Purpose: To align with the Law of Identical Harvest, creating a mental environment ripe for financial growth and prosperity.

What to do:

1. **Clear the weeds.** Write down all the blocked beliefs you have about money. These are the

"weeds" in your mental garden. Examples could be "Previous generations had it so easy. My generation has it so hard," "I'm not good with money," or "You have to work hard to get rich."

2. **Change the story.** For each blocked belief, write a counter-statement that turns it into a positive affirmation. For instance, "Money is the root of all evil" can be flipped to "Money is a tool for good." Or "I'm not good with money" can be changed into "I am learning to manage money wisely for my well-being and prosperity."

3. **Plant your seeds.** Close your eyes and relax your mind. Now, mentally plant each of your positive affirmations in your mental garden. Imagine each affirmation as a seed that you are planting in fertile soil. Visualize them growing into lush, fruitful trees.

4. **Water and nurture.** Throughout the day, "water" your mental garden with positive thoughts about money and abundance. Whenever you catch yourself reverting back to a blocked belief, pause and consciously replace it with its positive counter-statement. Feel the positive emotion as if these affirmations are your current reality.

5. **Have a dedicated harvest time.** At the end of each week, take some time to reflect on any changes in your financial situation or your attitude toward money. Celebrate all wins, whether it's receiving an opportunity or feeling less stressed about finances.

Your Law of Identical Harvest Decree

I am the master of my thoughts, the sower of my seeds, and the creator of my reality. I recognize that my thoughts are the seeds that I sow, and my life is the field in which they grow.

I plant these seeds in the fertile soil of my mind, and water them with feelings of joy, gratitude, and love. I know that the seeds I plant today will become my harvest of tomorrow, and I eagerly await the bounty that will come forth. I trust the natural process of growth, understanding that my seeds will sprout, grow, and flourish in perfect timing.

With every thought, I am sowing seeds. With every action, I am watering them. With every moment, I am nurturing my chosen seeds, knowing that they will bear the fruit of my desires.

I share my experiences and the fruits of my harvest with others. I rejoice in their successes and their harvests, knowing that we are all interconnected and that their joy is my joy.

With every moment, I am nurturing my chosen seeds, knowing that they will bear the fruit of my desires.

Your Law of Identical Harvest Journal Questions

- What seeds have you been sowing in your thoughts and emotions that could have led to your current outcomes?
- What seeds of intention, belief, and action can you plant now to manifest and ensure a bountiful harvest?
- How can you use the Law of Identical Harvest to change the course of your life by planting new seeds of positivity, love, and abundance?

THE MYSTERY OF QUIBBLES

It would poison you if you ate it because you have quibbles.
But you see, I can eat everything because I have no quibbles.

— *Abdullah*

Quibbles. It might sound like a silly little word, but these slight objections or criticisms about "the small stuff" can slow down our manifesting. Think of a garden hose (like the janky one in my garden): when it's pinched just a little, water still flows but at a slower pace. The more you pinch or squeeze, the harder it is for the water to pass. Quibbles function like this, slowly restricting the free flow of our desires and manifestations.

Neville was proud of his disciplined vegetarian diet, which was also devoid of alcohol and sweets. After his trip to Barbados he gifted Abdullah two luxurious bottles of the best Barbados brandy from his father. To Neville's surprise, within a week, the bottles were empty! He thought Abdullah would drink them over a year.[31]

Abdullah asked jokingly, "Say . . . How long do you expect those things to last?"[32]

Another time, Neville watched in shock as Abdullah tucked into a huge meaty dinner and ended his meal with a large bowl of ice cream.

As Neville explained, "He would sit down and polish off this enormous meal and wash it down with ale, precede it with three shots of rye (whiskey), and here was a man truly of the spirit."[33]

Baffled, Neville asked, "Ab, how can you do this?"

Abdullah, with a knowing smile, replied, "You couldn't do it; it would make you sick, because you have quibbles."

Abdullah was pointing out that Neville's stringent guidelines about what to eat and drink were self-imposed barriers. Abdullah knew this struggle intimately. Abdullah was raised in a strict orthodox family, and had been a vegetarian himself for forty years. He diligently adhered to all the traditional rules, but then underwent a profound transformation later in life. His awakening led him to esoteric knowledge that went beyond his initial religious practices.

Abdullah said to Neville, "I am not going to tell you 'you are crazy,' Neville, but you are, you know. All these things are stupid."[34]

Neville's father owned a general store, so he grew up eating everything. He came to New York at seventeen and fell into what he describes as "a state called John the Baptist." He says that in this state, a person "does violence to his appetite." In this state he became a strict vegan, celibate, and a nondrinker.

The "John the Baptist Phase" symbolizes a point in your spiritual quest focused on self-denial, self-restraint, and curbing your desires. During this time, you might hold back your appetites or natural urges as a form of self-control or spiritual cleansing. In contrast, the next stage, often likened to the "Jesus Phase," encourages you to welcome life's joys and desires. Moving through these spiritual phases helps you find a balanced and harmonious way to manifest your wants and needs.[35]

As Neville said:

> "My friend Abdullah who taught me this story, he was in it for forty years. He hadn't touched anything that was meat, especially pork. He was born and raised in the Jewish faith, and for forty years he touched nothing that was meat. But certainly he, not only forty years, but from the time of birth up until he was almost eighty years old, he hadn't touched pork. And then came the same thing to him that happened to me."[36]

To explain his point, Abdullah told a story from the Bible's book of Acts. In the story, Peter sees all kinds of animals and food coming down from the sky. When a voice from heaven tells him to eat, Peter says he can't because the food isn't clean. The voice answers, "What I have made clean, you must not call unclean."

This meant that everything in life is here for us to enjoy, and by seeing certain things as "bad," we limit ourselves.

This was a life-changing lesson for Neville. He realized that our quibbles—about food, money, relationships, or anything else—are often just our own fears and judgments showing up and holding us back.

Here's the other thing about quibbles (aka self made barriers): they can really mess with our ability to manifest. Manifesting is all about believing in endless possibilities and trusting the Divine to flow through us, right? Well, when we hold onto these quibbles, it's like we're giving mixed manifesting messages. We're trying to bring our desires into reality, but at the same time, we're holding on to beliefs that block them. This kind of tug-of-war inside of us makes manifesting feel so hard sometimes.

That's why it's so important to get to know our quibbles. Quibbles are not facts of life; they're just beliefs we've picked up along the way. When we spot them, we're one step closer to letting them go.

So, for you, here's the question: Can you get rid of your quibbles? Can you see that they're just your own fears stopping you from enjoying life?

It's not just about food. It's about understanding that our quibbles—whether about diet, finances, relationships, or any aspect of life—are manifestations of our fears and self-judgments. Sometimes it's hard to believe that these small things can hold us back. These self-made barriers limit our experiences and impact our ability to manifest our true desires. By compartmentalizing certain things as "good" or "bad," we're narrowing our lens of perception and joy.

Quibbles aren't innate truths. They're accumulated beliefs. Recognizing them means we're a step closer to freeing ourselves. So, ask yourself: Are you pinching your hose of life with quibbles?

Choosing to release them paves the way for manifestation. All the wonderful things you crave (desire) lie just beyond these self-imposed barriers. Recognizing, understanding, and lovingly setting them aside will create space for more love, wealth, joy, and life.

Ego-Driven Health and Spiritual Practices: Coming out of the Graveyard

You're so good, you're good for nothing. And you're trying to get into the kingdom by being good. You don't eat meat, no kind of meat, you don't drink any alcoholic liquor, so you're so good. And you're celibate at the age that you are today. And so all the fires you've bottled up in you, trying to be good.

— *Abdullah*

As I'm typing this, I can't help but think about my own choices. I don't eat meat, drink, or smoke anything, and I've even opted for celibacy right now. Like Abdullah in his younger days, I have never experienced pork. I have also never had coffee. On the surface, these seem like clean, healthy choices, and they mostly are. They make me feel good, both physically and morally. But here's the kicker: Are these choices really about health, or am I secretly trying to be "holier than thou"?

You see, I've been hanging out with Abdullah, who taught me about quibbles. Sure, it's great to live a life that aligns with our values. But what if these values or beliefs are limiting my life experience? What if they're my quibbles?

So, what does "holy" even mean to me? In our current world, healthy is the new holy. Is it about setting up a bunch of don'ts and can'ts, or is it more about aligning with what feels authentically right for me?

Don't get me wrong. My choices have given me a sense of clarity, peace, and purpose. But here's the thing: could I be blocking myself from other amazing experiences because of these so-called "holy" rules I've set? Maybe it's time to really question these quibbles. I was once a raw vegan and had to release it because it was unhealthy for my body.

I don't have all the answers yet, and that's okay. This is a journey, after all. Each day presents a new opportunity for learning, growth, and self-reflection. I'm learning to ask these questions, to challenge my beliefs, to explore my quibbles.

And I invite you to do the same. Let's question our quibbles, challenge our self-imposed limitations, and embrace what life has to offer.

Neville had been living a spartan life for years, avoiding many of life's pleasures. He believed that such self-discipline made him more spiritually pure. But Abdullah saw things differently. He believed that our self-imposed restrictions, or quibbles, often become obstacles to our personal and spiritual growth. He felt that Neville's abstention from certain things was a quibble. Abdullah believed that the world, with all its pleasures, is not inherently good or bad. It is the barriers we construct within ourselves that limit our experiences. These were the words of Abdullah, after Neville manifested the trip to Barbados:

> After you have proven this law, you will become normal, Neville. You will come out of that graveyard, you will come out of that dead past where you think you are being holy. For all you are really doing, you know, you are being so good, Neville, you are good for nothing.

This concept, "coming out of the graveyard," is a powerful metaphor used by Abdullah to describe the state of self-imposed restrictions and stagnation. In this context, the "graveyard" represents a place where growth and progress are halted—a state of lifelessness, where we rigidly adhere to certain rules or beliefs that hold us back from living a full and vibrant life.

By telling Neville to come out of the graveyard, Abdullah was urging him to break free from restrictive beliefs and behaviors. When Neville returned to New York, he let go of his ascetic ways, including abstaining from alcohol and smoking, which he had believed were essential for spiritual development. He embraced a more relaxed lifestyle.

Abdullah's message is a reminder that neither spiritual growth nor manifestation necessarily come from self-imposed purity or self-denial. Instead, it's embracing the freedom to live an enjoyable life while still being connected to the Divine.

So let's ask ourselves, are we holding on to quibbles that restrict us from fully experiencing life? Are we living in a metaphorical graveyard of our own making? It's time to examine our beliefs, let go of self-imposed limitations, and embrace life with open arms. Let's come out of the graveyard and live life to the fullest.

Your pathway to manifesting your desires becomes clearer when you unpinch the hose and let life flow.

Recognizing Our Quibbles

Let's dive into some typical areas where quibbles sneak in. For starters, how about money? Ever catch yourself thinking you need to break your back to earn a decent living or that spiritual folks can't be rich? These are classic money quibbles that block your financial flow.

And what about love? Ever feel like all the great partners are already snatched up, or that you need to compromise your soul to make a relationship work? Yep, those are love quibbles, roadblocks to meaningful connections.

Or perhaps you think you're too old to pursue a new dream or that life has to be hard. These self-limiting blocked beliefs, my friends, are personal growth quibbles that keep you from blossoming into your best self.

Notice anything familiar? The first step to breaking free is spotting these self-imposed barriers. We all have them, and they're not inherently bad—just blocked beliefs we've unwittingly adopted. The real magic begins when we question their usefulness.

Picture your life without these restrictions. It's like suddenly seeing in full color. Free from quibbles, you'll find a broader, more vibrant world full of opportunities that were always there but were hidden by your old views.

Without relationship roadblocks, love becomes more natural and fulfilling. No more preconceived notions that relationships must be hard; instead, you find balance and mutual respect.

Unburdened by money quibbles, you invite financial abundance. Gone is the guilt or the false notion that money and spirituality can't coexist. You're open to prosperity, plain and simple.

And say good-bye to the blocked beliefs holding back your personal growth. Age and past experiences become irrelevant as you embrace your untapped potential.

The point is, letting go of these quibbles opens up a whole new realm of possibilities. It's as if you've stepped into a room filled with all the good stuff you've ever wanted—only now you're not holding yourself back.

By shedding these limitations, you align yourself with your desires, making it that much easier for them to materialize. Ultimately, a life without quibbles is a life where you're free to follow your dreams, expand your horizons, and embrace experiences that once seemed out of reach.

So, keep questioning, keep growing, and most importantly, keep opening yourself to life's endless opportunities. Trust me, you're worth it!

Your Quibbles Decree

I deserve the best life has to offer.

Today, I control of my own fate.

No longer will I allow minor objections to shape my reality or restrict my path. I am not bound by past fears or perceived limitations, for they are merely shadows cast by my former self. Today, I choose to step into the sunlight of my potential, leaving those shadows behind.

I deserve the best life has to offer, and any quibbles that suggest otherwise are merely illusions that I am ready to dispel. Today, I choose to see beyond these illusions, to the abundance that life has to offer.

I commit myself to self-discovery, growth, and unbounded potential.

Just as I am, I am enough. In fact, I am not just enough, I am more than enough, and I have everything I need within me to achieve my greatest dreams.

This is my pledge to myself, not just for today, but for every day. I deserve the best life has to offer.

Your Quibbles Journal Questions

- Identify a quibble (self-imposed limitation) that currently exists in your life. What purpose does this quibble serve to you?

- How would it feel to live without self-imposed limitations?
- Envision your life without any quibbles. How would it change?

THE MYSTERY OF DEATH AND REBIRTH

You will die but you will not surely die.

— ABDULLAH

Abdullah said to Neville before he left for Barbados on that impactful trip, "So you're going to Barbados. May I tell you, you're going to die but you will not surely die . . . but you will die."[37] Neville assumed he meant physical death and that he was going to die on his trip.

Neville left, puzzled by this cryptic message. He said, "Well, I went off thinking, well, I'll die, die in Barbados. I didn't die in Barbados but I died: I died to everything that I was doing." In Barbados, he spent three months attending parties and gatherings but abstained from consuming any meat or alcohol. It was a practice he had observed for seven years. When he boarded the ship to return to New York, he found himself seated at a dinner table with several others. In contrast to his usual habits, he indulged in wine, soup, fish, and meat. Every restraint he had observed for seven years, he cast aside in one night and continued this way for the remainder of his trip.

Neville later realized that this was what Abdullah meant. He had died to his old habits, the self-imposed restrictions that had bound him for seven years. This was a metaphorical death, a shedding of old beliefs, quibbles, and patterns of behavior, making way for a new sense of freedom and self-awareness.

By shedding his old self-concept and embracing a new sense of freedom, Neville was able to more profoundly understand and apply the spiritual principles he taught.

Metaphorical death signifies the letting go of old identities, beliefs, and limitations, making way for a new, more empowered self to emerge. In the process of manifesting your desires, metaphorical death has a key role. It helps us overcome the barriers of blocked beliefs and preconceived notions that hold us back from actualizing our dreams and aspirations.

This idea is about "metaphorical death," which means letting go of our old ways of thinking that hold us back and embracing a new way of thinking that helps us reach our goals and be our best selves.

As humans in earth school, we often find ourselves deeply attached to (or addicted to) the identities we constructed or those that have been shaped by our experiences. These identities, as comfy as they may be, can be barriers to growth and manifesting. To truly step into your power, it's necessary to let go of, or 'die' to, the old versions of yourself. This process is not about losing who you are. It's about shedding the layers that no longer serve you. It's a rebirth, an awakening to a more empowered you. As you embrace transformation, you must hold onto the new identities that align with your aspirations. This shift in identity is not just a change; it's a rebirth.

There Is No Death

Abdullah referred to physical death as putting the body back where he picked it up.

When it comes to actual death, Neville taught that death did not exist. He believed that what we perceive as death is just a transition to another state of existence or consciousness. He taught that life is eternal, and death is merely an illusion.

He argued that everyone is a manifestation of the divine and that we're all interconnected, part of the same infinite consciousness. This idea aligns with some traditions that view life and death as part of a continuous cycle or a progression of different states of consciousness.

It makes sense that Abdullah taught Neville this. There are spiritual traditions within Ethiopian thought that align with the idea that everyone is a manifestation of the divine and that we're all interconnected, part of the same infinite consciousness. In other words, connectedness between all living things and the spiritual world.

In many of these traditions, death is seen not as an end but as a transition to another form of existence or a change in the focus of consciousness. This perspective aligns with the concept that we are all part of an infinite consciousness, and death represents a change within this continuum.

Abdullah's energy is very much still alive. This book is a divine transmission directly from him. I feel his consciousness empowering me to share his wisdom with you. The dead are not dead.

Ethiopian spiritual traditions include Christianity, Judaism, Islam, and indigenous belief systems. Each of these traditions has elements that align with the idea that everyone is a manifestation of the divine and that we're all interconnected, part of the same infinite consciousness.

Disillusionment and the Dark Night of the Soul

Sometimes, life throws us a curveball that makes us question everything. This kind of death can feel like the rug has been pulled out from under us. Believe it or not, this feeling of disillusionment can be a good thing. It's like a wake-up call, making us reevaluate our beliefs, attitudes, and habits, and that can be the first step toward positive change.

"Ellie," one of my Spiritpreneur clients, always thought that having a lot of money would make her happy. But when she finally achieved financial success, she still felt empty and even more stressed. This feeling of disillusionment pushed her to rethink her ideas about success and happiness. Disillusionment became her powerful force for change.

The concept of dying to your old self to make way for a new self is tied to spiritual transformation. It's the process of breaking free from broken beliefs, habits, and self-identifications that no longer serve you, and welcoming in a new and more expansive way of being. This transformation often comes after periods of intense struggle or suffering, sometimes referred to as a "dark night of the soul."

The term "dark night of the soul" comes from a poem by the 16th-century Spanish mystic Saint John of the Cross. It's about a spiritual crisis in the path toward union with the Divine. In this stage, you might feel intense emotional pain, existential doubt, and a sense of separation from your higher self or the Divine. It's a period of purification where all the false beliefs, illusions, and attachments that you've accumulated over time come to the surface to be released.

This dark night is often characterized by feelings of emptiness, loneliness, despair, and a loss of meaning in life. You may feel like you're wandering in the wilderness, unable to find your way. This darkness is not a punishment. It's a necessary part of your spiritual path.

As you go through this intense inner transformation, your old self, with its outdated beliefs, self-identifications, and patterns of behavior, is dying. This process of dying to the old is necessary to make way for the new self to emerge, like a phoenix rising from the ashes.

In Greek mythology, the phoenix is a legendary bird that lives for hundreds of years. When its life cycle ends, it builds a nest, sets it on fire, and is consumed by the flames. From the ashes, a new phoenix arises, reborn and renewed.

In Christianity, the concept of resurrection is central. It signifies the victory of life over death, light over darkness, and the possibility of renewal and redemption. In the process of spiritual rebirth, you too can experience this resurrection, rising from the ashes of your old self, reborn with a new sense of purpose, direction, and connection to your higher self and the Divine.

Embracing Life's Offerings

Abdullah taught Neville the transformative narrative of "The One Greater Than John," meaning consciousness transformation from the state of John, restricted awareness, to the state of Jesus, expansive consciousness. After studying with Abdullah, Neville came away with the belief that, "Bibles are psychological dramas representing the consciousness of man."[38] I've taken both "Bible as Literature" and a "Bible as History" classes, so I find this thought process interesting.

As we discussed in the last chapter, Abdullah was a strict vegetarian for over 40 years, and, due to his faith, he had never consumed pork in his life. One night, God spoke to him in a vision, questioning his reluctance to eat the food offered to him by others while expecting them to partake in the food he offered. Abdullah was a teacher, and he had observed that his hosts would go out of their way to prepare meals tailored to his vegetarian and non-pork diet.[39]

Following this vision, Abdullah was invited to a banquet where he was the guest of honor. The main course was a roasted suckling pig with a sweet potato placed in its mouth. It was a delicacy that he had avoided for over 40 years.

Abdullah ate the pork, breaking with his orthodox beliefs and vegetarian principles. The divine message reminded him that if he wished for others to accept his teachings, he must also accept what they offered.

Abdullah's ability to embrace all aspects of life without restriction was part of his teaching. He understood that spiritual growth involves letting go of rigid beliefs and accepting life in its entirety. Abdullah lived to well over 100 and, as Neville was told, returned to his native Ethiopia to lay down the garment he had picked up a century before.

The Blessings of Rebirth

You see, one day the being that is really dreaming your life will awaken, and you will be enhanced beyond your wildest dreams because of your experiences.

— Neville

In this process of dying to the old and being reborn you may find that you're more in alignment with your true self and your soul's purpose. As you release the beliefs and identity that was holding you back, you'll be operating from a higher level of consciousness, where you're more attuned to the infinite possibilities and abundance available to you.

You might experience increased levels of joy, peace, love, and fulfillment. You also may find that you have a deeper connection to your intuition, greater clarity, and a more expansive understanding of yourself and the world around you.

While the dark night of the soul and the process of dying to the old self can be challenging (some of us may say horrific), it's a necessary part of your spiritual journey. Embrace the transformation and it will lead to a more expansive, free, and fulfilling life.

Allow yourself to undergo a metaphorical death. Let go of old beliefs and habits. This paves the way for your rebirth. It's like waking up with fresh eyes, feeling reinvigorated and renewed, ready to embrace life in a whole new way.

Shed the limitations of the past and create space for a more empowered and confident version of you. This new you is unburdened by old insecurities and fears and is free to explore and experience life fully.

Rebirth is not about forgetting the past or pretending that it never happened. It's about integrating your experiences and using them as stepping stones to manifesting your best self.

A Little Child Shall Lead Them

In 1933, Abdullah gave Neville a piece of paper with words that would leave a lasting impact: "The King of Kings, the Eternally-Becoming One, which men call Christ, must ever be remembered as a little child." Neville carefully placed this paper in an old Bible, preserving a key lesson from his mentor.

Abdullah was reminding Neville of the importance of maintaining an open, childlike heart throughout the process of transformation.

A child's approach to life is about being open, curious, and willing to embrace new experiences without skepticism or cynicism. Allow your "new self" to be born, free from past constraints and ready to manifest with childlike wonder.

Embracing a childlike approach means treating each day as an opportunity to experience life fresh and unburdoned, unburdened by the past. It means continuously growing, and remaining open.

Neville's Rebirth

Neville worked with Abdullah seven days a week for seven years. Neville wasn't able to pay Abdullah so he cleaned his apartment in exchange for the lessons. But I am pretty sure that Abdullah would have taught him anyway, as it was all divinely orchestrated.

Remember when Abdullah and Neville first "met," and Abdullah said he'd give Neville all the teachings he was meant to and then move on? Neville's friend Freedom Barry confirmed that Abdullah encouraged Neville to spread his wings: "So after Abdullah had decided that Neville had enough, and this was seven full years, he just closed his doors to everybody. He didn't take in the newspapers, he didn't take in the milk when it was delivered, and this was his way of telling Neville, 'You're out of the nest, you have to go, you have to do it.'"[40] Then Neville borrowed $5, rented a space, and presented his first lecture.

When he finally "graduated" from Abdullah, Neville's friend Israel Regardie describes it as, "he was able to loosen his hold upon the hem of Abdullah's skirt to become a teacher in his own right."[41] Neville had to die from his identity as Abdullah's student who cleaned his home in exchange for food and knowledge.

Concerning Abdullah's actual physical death, here's what Neville had to say:

> Abdullah? Lived to be over a hundred and had one consuming desire, to put the body back where he picked it up which was in Ethiopia. The last time I met Abdullah was about eight years ago in New York City. About seven years ago I met his secretary, and she voiced that request of his, and said he was planning to return to Ethiopia. I haven't seen or heard from Abdullah or the secretary since.[42]

Transformation and rebirth is an ongoing process. Abdullah's desire to return to Ethiopia reflects the cyclical nature of life and spiritual growth. In the same way that Abdullah sought to complete his cycle by returning to his homeland, we can view the process of metaphorical death and rebirth as a cyclical journey, with each cycle bringing us closer to our true self and our desires.

In Guyana, when someone visits us in our dreams after they have transitioned from this life, we say they dreamed us. It is not us who are dreaming them, but them dreaming us as a form of visitation. After my Uncle Steve died, he dreamed me, warning me to urgently get to his family in Brooklyn to look over the paperwork. I had no idea what paperwork he was worried about, but it turns out they were in the process of selling their homes.

Abdullah "dreamed" Neville after his physical death. He said that Abdullah, who was well over 80 when they met, appeared to him under 40, six inches taller, and in a Caucasian body. This was Neville's envisioning of him, "towering in this sheer majesty, and here, what he never wore on earth." Other than the physical, Neville said that the "majestic figure" had no change in identity.

It was still unmistakably Abdullah.

In the dream, Abdullah and Neville were discussing the theme of Neville's lecture for that night. Abdullah then showed him a small tape recorder and explained its purpose with these words:

> Now as you know, Neville, it only echoes; that's all that it can do. That's the world, the world is only mechanism, it's just mechanical. The whole vast world, the eternal structure of God's eternal world, all these garments they're just as mechanical as that. And now, you're not going to speak into it, you're only going to hear, you're going to listen, and what you listen to will play back there. What you listen to and hear from within you, as you actually hear it you'll play it back there.[43]

Abdullah used the tape recorder as a reminder that the world reflects our inner thoughts and beliefs. The world doesn't create new experiences for us; it just plays back what we imagine and assume within ourselves.

To demonstrate, Abdullah asked Neville to listen inwardly, to imagine hearing the sound of certain friends' voices. As Neville did this, Abdullah played back the imagined sounds on the tape recorder, even though no words had been spoken out loud. The tape recorder echoed the sounds Neville had imagined, just as the world echoes our inner beliefs and assumptions.

If we want to change our outer experiences, we must first change our inner thoughts and assumptions.

Metaphorical death involves shedding the blocked beliefs and self-imposed restrictions that hold us back from our full potential. This process of transformation and renewal gives us the opportunity to manifest a life that aligns with our true selves. The tape recorder in the dream reminds us that the key to unlocking this power is within us. As we shift our inner beliefs, we pave the way for a rebirth in our outer world.

What do you need to let die in your life?

How to Allow Your Old Self to Die

By allowing ourselves to undergo metaphorical death, we shed the skin of our past to be reborn into a new, more empowered state of being.

Here's how you can allow your old self to "die" and experience transformation:

- **Embrace change.** We resist change because it's uncomfortable, and it takes us out of our comfort zone. Instead of resisting it, embrace it. See it as an opportunity for growth and transformation.
- **Release attachments.** We often hold onto things, people, or situations that no longer serve us because we're attached to them. These attachments can hold us back and prevent us from moving forward. Releasing these attachments helps you free yourself from the past and make space for new experiences and opportunities.
- **Question your beliefs.** Many of our beliefs are formed during childhood or as a result of past experiences. They may not necessarily be true or serve us in our current situation. Question

your beliefs. Are they really true? Do they serve you? If not, it's time to let them go.

- **Forgive and let go.** Holding on to resentment, anger, or hurt only harms you. It keeps you stuck in the past and prevents you from moving forward. Forgive those who have hurt you, not for their sake, but for yours. Let go of the pain and the resentment.
- **Reinvent yourself.** After you've let go of the old, it's time to reinvent yourself. Who do you want to be? What kind of life do you want to live? Imagine the best version of yourself and start living as if you're already that person.
- **Trust the process.** Transformation can be challenging. It's not always a smooth process. There will be times when you feel lost or confused. That's okay. Know that it's all part of your growth.

By letting go of the old, you make space for the new. You become a more empowered, happier, and fulfilled version of yourself, capable of manifesting with ease.

Exercise: Lucid Dreaming: The Dreamscape Process

The dreamer in you is God. Tonight as you dream ask yourself where you are.

— NEVILLE

Purpose: To engage directly with your subconscious mind through lucid dreaming.

Lucid dreaming is when you become aware that you're dreaming while you're still asleep. In a lucid dream, you realize that everything around you is a creation of your own mind, and this awareness gives you the ability to control and change the dream. This practice aligns beautifully with metaphorical death and rebirth, because it can help you to identify and release old beliefs, confront fears, and embrace new possibilities within the safe confines of the dream state.

Lucid dreaming offers a space for personal growth, healing, and goal manifestation. It can give you an immersive experience of your desired reality. By taking control in a dream, you can intentionally create scenarios that align with your goals and intentions. This is a way to "program" your subconscious mind to manifest your desires in waking life.

As Neville says:

> In dream we are usually the servant of our vision rather than its master, but the internal fantasy of dream can be turned into an external reality. In dream, as in meditation, we slip from this world into a dimensionally larger world, and I know that the forms in dream are not flat

two-dimensional images which modern psychologists believe them to be.

In lucid dreaming, you can vividly and consciously manifest your desires. By creating ideal scenarios and immersing yourself in the emotions of your dreams, you align your subconscious mind and energy with your desired outcome, making it easier to manifest.

Lucid dreaming is a skill that may take some time to develop, but it is worth it as a powerful tool.

What to do:

1. **Set your intention.** Before going to bed, set a clear intention that you want to become aware and take control in your dreams. Repeat a simple statement, such as "Tonight, I will become aware that I am dreaming and I will take control."
2. **Relax.** As you lie down in bed, take a few moments to relax your body and quiet your mind. Engage in a short meditation, focusing on your breath and letting go of any tension or stress.
3. **Visualize your desired dream.** In your relaxed state, begin to imagine the dream world you would like to experience. Create a vivid mental image of the environment, objects, and sensations you want to experience.
4. **Pay attention to dream objects.** Once you find yourself in a dream, pay close attention to any inanimate or stationary objects (e.g., a chair, table, stairway, or tree). Become aware of their three-dimensional reality and physicality.
5. **Take hold of an object and command yourself to wake up.** When you notice that you are dreaming, reach out and grab one of the

objects in your dream. As you firmly hold onto it, mentally command yourself to awake with the intention of becoming fully conscious and in control of the dream.

6. **Awaken in the dream.** As you awaken within the dream, you will find yourself in a new sphere of consciousness. You will be fully conscious and in control of your attention, able to shape and direct the dream as you wish.
7. **Explore and manifest.** In this lucid state, explore the dream world, interact with the environment, and bring your desired manifestations to life. Embrace the emotions and sensations that accompany your creations, knowing that this experience is helping to bring them into your waking reality.
8. **Reflect and journal.** When you wake up, reflect on your experience. Write down the details of the dream, your feelings, and any insights you gained. Over time, this practice will strengthen your ability to lucid dream and manifest your desires.

Your Death and Rebirth Decree

I rise from the ashes like a phoenix.

As I release my blocked beliefs, self-doubt, and self-denial, I open up space for transformation and renewed life.

My old self must die so that my new self can be reborn.

I rise from the ashes like a phoenix.

I embrace my new self with open arms. I welcome the changes and transformations, knowing that they bring me the life I desire.

In this process of rebirth, I let go of my past and welcome my future with gratitude, grace, and joy. I rise from the ashes like a phoenix. With each day that passes, I grow closer to my goals, moving forward with confidence and a purpose.

I am supported and guided by the divine spirit within. !

Your Death and Rebirth Journal Questions

- Consider a time when you've experienced a "metaphorical death," leaving behind old habits or beliefs to embrace a new way of thinking or being. How did it impact you?
- Have you ever experienced a "dark night of the soul," a period of intense internal struggle or disillusionment? How did this challenging time help you with growth or transformation?
- What new beliefs or attitudes have you embraced that have empowered you to create positive changes in your life?

THE MYSTERY OF EXTRASENSORY PERCEPTION

You have forgotten. We were in China together thousands of years ago, but you promised to completely forget in order to play the part you must play now.

— *Abdullah*

During Dr. Murphy's first encounter with Abdullah, he made a startling revelation. Abdullah stated confidently that Murphy was not one of five children, as he'd always believed, but one of six. They had never met or interacted before. Murphy had grown up knowing only four siblings, and he had no reason to believe his family was larger.

Murphy was a pharmacist, ordained priest, and minister born in Ireland. He studied Hindu doctrines with sages in India. Dr. Murphy wrote over 30 books.

Baffled, Murphy went to his mother. Abdullah was correct. Murphy indeed had another brother, a sibling who was stillborn. The family had chosen not to speak of him. This brother's existence had remained a family secret.

This revelation opened Murphy's eyes to a new realm of spiritual understanding. His meeting with Professor

Abdullah, followed by this discovery, marked a turning point in his spiritual journey.

Beyond being psychic, Abdullah was deeply connected, providing a testament to the breadth of his consciousness. He was psychic and telepathic, he could astral travel and use his dreams, he was able to channel or receive divine inspiration, and he had past life recall.

Guess what? You own a magic tool kit filled with presents that you didn't even know you had. This is what I call our "extrasensory gifts." They're like magic powers, encompassing everything from telepathy and psychic awareness to remembering past lives and astral travel. These aren't just party tricks. These extraordinary gifts are keys to manifesting and consciously creating your life on a whole new level.

The term ESP (extrasensory perception) was commonly used back in the day to encompass a range of phenomena related to intuitive abilities and experiences. ESP referred to the ability to perceive or access information beyond the five physical senses. Telepathy, psychic abilities, and astral travel are all considered forms of ESP. These gifts allow us to tap into intuitive, energetic, and spiritual realms, expanding their perception and understanding of the world around them. While the term ESP is not commonly used today, the concept still encompasses these extraordinary abilities.

Abdullah embodied the power of extrasensory perception. His psychic abilities were so pronounced, he seemed to anticipate things with incredible precision. When Abdullah met Neville for the first time he said, "Neville, you are six months late. The Brothers told me you would be here six months ago. I will remain until you have received all that I must give you. Then I will depart." Neville was shocked, as they had never met before.

Abdullah's mastery of astral travel no doubt allowed him to journey beyond the confines of the physical world, proving that our reality is not limited to what we can touch or see. By harnessing the power of extrasensory perception, we too can step into a world of expanded consciousness and infinite possibilities.

The beauty of these gifts is how they bring you closer to the essence of who you really are and what you can do. They reveal the seamless flow of energy within and around you, and remind you of your endless potential. Energy isn't something we create or destroy; it's something we harness and channel.

These extrasensory gifts remind us that everything—yes, everything—is possible. We're only limited by our imagination.

How cool is that?

Consider the gift of intuition, which we all have access to. When you're consciously manifesting, maintain a strong connection with your intuition. Your inner guidance can direct you toward actions that align with your desires and provide insight into anything blocking your progress.

Expanding our awareness and understanding of the "clairs" can significantly enhance our ability to manifest. The clairs are various types of psychic abilities that correspond to our senses. Each clair represents a unique pathway to receive intuitive guidance, which can provide invaluable insight when it comes to conscious creation.

Clairvoyance (clear seeing) allows individuals to visualize beyond the physical realm; clairaudience (clear hearing) involves receiving intuitive information through sounds; clairsentience (clear feeling) encompasses receiving psychic information through feelings or sensations; claircognizance (clear knowing) is characterized by a sudden, clear understanding of something; clairgustance (clear tasting) involves experiencing tastes without eating or drinking anything; and clairalience (clear smelling) pertains to detecting non-physical scents as messages or signs.

For example, someone with a developed sense of clairvoyance might visualize their goals more vividly, adding depth and detail to their manifestation practice. A clairaudient, on the other hand, might hear intuitive messages in songs or sounds. Clairsentients may feel physical sensations that guide their choices, while claircognizants may suddenly "know" the steps they need to take.

Developing these psychic abilities allows us to enhance our manifesting process by aligning our actions with the guidance we receive intuitively. These abilities remind us that we're intimately connected and capable of manifesting our deepest desires by tapping into and trusting this expansive universal wisdom.

The more we can understand and nurture our clair abilities, the more effectively we can manifest. These abilities, or channels of intuitive information, can help us align our thoughts, emotions, and actions with the energetic flow of God consciousness, helping turn our dreams into reality.

Beware of Misplaced Faith

An older woman who connected with Abdullah in Atlantic City had been advised that he had the power to inflict harm on a man in her neighborhood. She approached him with an offer of $300 (lots of money at the time) to bring destruction to her neighbor.

Abdullah said to her, "My dear, whoever advised you this way is silly. God is love, just love. First of all, if I had that power I wouldn't use it, not in that direction, and secondly, it isn't."

Immediately the woman thought less of Abdullah. She went to another so-called spiritual master, a neighbor of Abdullah's who Neville called a "phony of phonies," who gladly accepted the $300. Neville used this story to illustrate how such fraudsters thrive, exploiting people's beliefs and fears.[44]

What Is Reincarnation?

> [Abdullah] said, "For six months ago [the brothers] told me to expect Neville, Neville's coming, and you mustn't leave the city until Neville has received all that you must give him. When you go, he must carry on." And here was this man . . . I never saw him before . . . I couldn't remember him. Then he said, "You have no memory, but it'll come back, it'll all come back."[45]

In the beginning, Neville was hesitant to meet with Abdullah. He delayed their first meeting until he could no longer find an excuse. When they met, Abdullah greeted Neville by name. When Neville expressed his confusion, Abdullah responded, "Oh yes, you do know me, but you have forgotten. We were together in China thousands of years ago, but you pledged to completely forget in order to fulfill the role you must play now."

So what roles have you pledged to play?

A woman wrote a letter about an experience during one of Neville's lectures. As she watched him on the platform, she didn't see Neville as he was. She saw an ancient Chinese philosopher. This visual shift was persistent throughout his entire talk. Reflecting upon this, she recalled a psychic experience from years prior. In this vision, she had been led by the same ancient Chinese scholar to a cavern, where they witnessed a cocoon breaking open on a granite stone, releasing a mixture of water and colorful oil that exuded a sensation of rising heat. After this revealing experience, the ancient figure guided her back to her group, who hadn't noticed her temporary departure.

Connecting the dots, she realized that Neville was wearing the face of the ancient philosopher from her past experience. This is the same truth Abdullah had shared with Neville in 1931. Even though Neville had no recollection of it, he understood the concept. He believed he had emptied himself of all past memories to undertake the journey of human life faithfully, assuring himself that his origin and his destiny were one and the same.

Neville took this as a reminder that every part must be lived, every role must be played in the grand scheme of existence. As he saw it, it was like an actor fully investing themselves in their character, living each role with conviction.

Reincarnation is the philosophical or religious concept that an individual's soul is reborn in a new body after death. This cycle of birth, death, and rebirth continues over many lifetimes, and is a central tenet in various belief systems, including those of the Igbo, Yoruba, and Zulu, and in Hinduism, Buddhism, and certain New Age philosophies.

The process of reincarnation is often linked with the universal law of karma, suggesting that the actions taken in a person's life can influence their fate in a future life.

Reincarnation is a path for spiritual evolution and learning. The soul voluntarily chooses to forget its divine origins to fully experience and learn from the human condition in each lifetime. The ultimate goal of this cyclical experiment is to play every part, to learn every lesson, and to eventually remember your true, divine nature.

How to Use Extrasensory Gifts for Manifesting

- **Amplifying Intuition:** Trust your intuitive guidance. Use your intuition to navigate choices and align with desires that are in alignment with your highest good.
- **Visualization and Imagination:** Tap into the realm of astral travel and connect with higher dimensions to expand your imaginative powers. Use astral experiences to vividly visualize and create detailed mental images of your desires.
- **Past Life Insights:** Explore reincarnation to gain insights into your past lives. Discover any patterns or unresolved issues. Heal and release any blocked beliefs or karmic imprints to open up new possibilities.
- **Co-Creation with Spirit Guides:** Engage in dialogues with your spirit guides, who can offer guidance and support with your manifesting. Utilize your psychic abilities to establish a clear channel of communication and receive insight from Divine Source Energy.

- **Vibrational Alignment:** Use your extrasensory gifts to attune to the vibrational frequency of your desires. By aligning your energy with the frequency of what you wish to manifest, you accelerate manifestations.
- **Astral Manifestation:** Harness astral travel to explore parallel realities and observe potential outcomes. Engage in conscious astral manifestations by planting intentions in the astral realm and allowing them to ripple into your physical reality.

Exercise: Meditative Words for Personal Power

Purpose: *To harness the power of words in your manifestation practice.*

Message of a Master by John McDonald, written in 1929, is suspected by many to be about Abdullah. It's the story of a man who encounters a Master Teacher on a quest for the Law of Life. The many parallel details and lessons are clear, although Abdullah is not mentioned as the master by name.

In the book, "Abdullah" (even though it's most likely our Abdullah, I will put quotes around his name) directs the man to meditate on 35 different words every evening, for 30 minutes to an hour. Here are the instructions he gives:

> After the day's activities devoted to your ordinary duties and affairs and the consequent devitalization of your life force, more or less, it is well to set apart an hour or half hour, as your judgment might dictate, each evening when you can be

> alone and undisturbed, and in the quiet and stillness of your own being, take each word separately down the list, or if you feel so disposed, select such words from the list as you feel your particular needs require at the time. ***Firmly impress your being*** with each word and at the same time, interpreting its meaning and its effect upon you, not necessarily in the terms of its generally accepted meaning, but strictly as it appeals to you.

"Abdullah" advised him to focus on the meditation and not get hung up on the words. He says that the words will not only "keep the life force nourished, but also to bear you up, sustain and carry you through whenever the strength each particular word creates, is needed."

What to do:

1. **Set the scene.** Every evening, after your daily tasks, find a quiet half hour to an hour when you can be by yourself without interruptions.
2. **Choose your words.** Go through the provided list of power words. Either contemplate each word one by one, or pick specific words that resonate with your current needs.
3. **Immerse yourself in the word.** As you focus on each word, deeply feel its meaning and influence on you. Understand it in your personal context, not just its general definition.

4. **Adjust your attitude.** You hold the power in your life. Stand confidently in this truth. However, avoid using the declaration "I AM" with these words unless you're in a completely positive state of mind. Just stating the word without attaching "I AM" to it helps prevent your outer mind from doubting or denying its truth.

5. **Avoid mental distractions.** It's natural for your mind to wander. When it does, gently bring your focus back to the word you're meditating on. Over time, you'll become better at concentration.

6. **Stay relaxed.** This exercise should be effortless. Don't stress or overthink.

7. **Be consistent.** Make this a daily practice, unless certain unavoidable duties come up. Let these words slowly cleanse your mindset, much like drops of pure water purifying a dirty vessel.

8. **Detach from results.** Treat this practice like eating—you don't monitor immediate results from each meal. Similarly, allow these words to work their magic subconsciously. Just practice each evening and leave the words behind till the next session.

9. **Trust the process.** These affirmations, like nutrients, will find their way into your core, influencing positive change over time. You might not see immediate results, but they're silently reshaping your inner world and, in turn, your external reality.

Power Words

concentration	health
peace	strength
poise	energy
harmony	activity
good-will	vitality
nonresistance	power
justice	life
freedom	youth
guidance	success
wisdom	happiness
understanding	alertness
inspiration	resourcefulness
intelligence	persistence
memory	purpose
law and order	achievement
faith	mastery
confidence	dominion
spirit	

Your ESP Decree

I am an intuitive genius, a receiver of wisdom that transcends earthly understanding. In the still moments of reflection, I listen, for I am always guided. The whispers of my ancestors and the divine speak to me, guiding me along paths unseen.

I am an intuitive genius, and I trust this gift completely. I allow it to lead me, to guide me, to inspire me. It is more than a mere feeling; it is a knowing, a certainty that resonates within me. This truth empowers me to reach beyond my limitations, to grasp the unseen.

I am an intuitive genius, and every day I hone this ability. My intuition is a sacred tool, my unique key to unlocking the secrets of existence. I wield this gift with responsibility, humility, and grace.

In my interactions, in my decisions, and in my dreams, my intuition guides me, whispers to me, and comforts me. It is never wrong, for it is connected to a higher understanding, a knowing that transcends human comprehension. I am an intuitive genius, and I will never forsake this gift. I will honor it, nurture it, and allow it to flourish. It is a part of me, a sacred bond with the infinite, a continuous thread weaving through the quilt of life.

In the quiet moments of contemplation, in the decisions I face, in the dreams I pursue, I will remember always that I am an intuitive genius. This is my truth, my power, my destiny.

Your ESP Journal Questions

- How has extrasensory perception shown up in your life?
- What steps can you take to develop and enhance your ESP abilities?
- How has my intuition guided me to make decisions that led to manifesting my goals?

CONCLUSION: WHAT ABDULLAH WANTS YOU TO KNOW NOW

Take possession of your divine heritage.

— *Abd Allah*, And It Was Told of a Certain Potter

My Dear One,

Listen closely, for I speak with the certainty of experience. If you seek to manifest your dreams, you must be willing to die to your old self, to your old limitations and beliefs that have held you captive. It's not enough to merely wish or hope for change. You must demand it of yourself.

The world does not owe you anything, and when doubts and fears creep in, as they inevitably will, stand firm in your conviction that you are worthy of your dreams.

The only limits that exist are the ones you place on yourself. So, break free from the prison of your own making.

Be open to receiving. Your dreams are yours for the taking. Now, go and claim the life you were meant to live.

Praise to the unity of unities that is our unity; one in all and all in one.

Your Teacher

Walter C. Lanyon may not be widely recognized today but he was a prolific early 20th-century author and New Thought movement spiritual teacher. His writings focused on the transformational power of thought and our divine nature. He is also rumored to be one of Abdullah's students. His books *And It Was Told of a Certain Potter and Abd Allah, Teacher, Healer and Embers* are said to be about Abdullah.

One of the stories in *And It Was Told of a Certain Potter* is about "Abd Allah," the wise potter (and possibly an homage to Abdullah) and a widow named Maza.

Maza lives in a humble hut in Jerusalem and works hard cleaning the temple. Despite her efforts, she is poor in wealth and poorer in mind. "So poor was she in spirit that she could not even lift her eyes to the heavens and feast her hungry soul on the beauty so lavishly displayed." She desperately seeks Abd Allah's guidance, asking, "I AM burdened with poverty; wilt tell me of riches?"

We've all been like Maza at some point—unable to even count our blessings. We become trapped in a state that blocks us from experiencing any abundance already present.

Abd Allah tells Maza about fishermen unable to catch fish due to their blocked beliefs. They were told by the "voice of Truth" to cast their nets to the opposite side to succeed.[46] "Now, literally, to cast their nets on the right side would be casting them in the same waters they had fished all night, but they knew that to cast their nets on the right side was merely a command to change their thought from one of limitation to abundance."

It's not the physical waters that changed, but their internal state—their belief in what was possible. Once the fishermen shifted their beliefs from lack to prosperity, they were able to tap into the divine law of supply. Their desires were within their reach all along.

According to Abd Allah, "Supply is a law of God. He is Who created you, and He is responsible for you." You are a manifestation of divine energy. Abundance is your natural state. Free yourself to experience and enjoy the prosperity that has always been yours by divine right.

Sometimes people get stuck waiting for abundance to find them. Abd Allah advises: "Action is the law of progress. It is necessary to give out joy and happiness and not stand with our vessels full meekly waiting for someone to come to us."

For a long time that was me, standing with my vessel full, waiting for somebody to save me. Stop waiting.

You've learned to focus inwardly, to change your internal state. Here is another layer. Once you tune your inner frequency to what you want to manifest, radiate that frequency out into the world through meaningful action. Inspired action is leaving your meditation pillow to actually live your life.

Our Abdullah took purposeful action by coming to New York, by sitting in prime seats at the opera, by learning the Kabbalah and Greek, by teaching classes and seeing clients, by choosing Neville Goddard to share his teachings, and by deciding when to return to Ethiopia.

When we shift our thoughts, we change our reality. The scarcity that surrounds us is often a reflection of our inner thoughts. By changing the direction of our "nets," or thoughts, we invite plenty into our lives.

Abundance isn't something to be achieved. It is a state to be recognized by you. So, I ask you, do you believe in divine supply?

You're not a spectator waiting for good things to happen—you have the power to create those good things.

You don't need to attract abundance; you can create it from within.

You're already full of possibilities and potential. The good things you're looking for outside of you? They start inside. Your goals and dreams aren't just wishes; they're what you're meant to fulfill.

You're not stuck with whatever situations are happening. Change your life by creating from within. Obstacles are not roadblocks. They are your sacred opportunities to birth something new.

Your imagination isn't bound by what already exists. You have the power to think bigger, to go beyond what's known into what could be.

Make your vision a reality by believing it's possible. This is your time.

Your imagination births reality.

Door slam.

BONUS: THE PROCESSES

I have said all that I have to say.

— Abdullah[1]

Greetings, Esteemed Reader,

This section presents to you a series of transformative treatments, techniques, and exercises, carefully designed to lead you through the stages of conscious creation.

In my lifetime of study, I have come to realize that mastery of one's world is not an intellectual understanding, but a practiced art.

These processes offer you the tools necessary to apply the 13 Manifesting Scrolls. I assure you that your efforts shall not go unrewarded; for as you persevere in the execution of these processes, the world around you shall transform.

May you discover your infinite potential. And may you come to recognize your true self, as the masterful creator of your own reality.

With respect and affection,

Your Teacher

Abdullah closed each of his sessions with this prayer: "Praise be to that unity which is our unity, one in all and all in one."

It is a reminder that we are all one, and the unity that underpins everything. We are all connected. It is with this sense of unity, oneness, and love for the greater good that we approach manifesting.

Manifestation is more than just getting our individual desires. Manifesting is the art of aligning ourselves with the Divine force and becoming one with our intentions.

Manifesting is simple. We've all been doing it without realizing it since we were born. (Some would say we were manifesting before we were born.) Conscious manifesting is learning how to do it on purpose.

The core of the Law of Life says conscious manifesting is believing, really believing, that what you want is already yours. So, if you want to manifest something, you don't need a fancy technique. Just believe it's already yours.

If you come to the table with a lifetime of experiences, misaligned beliefs, old baggage and stuff, like most humans, conscious manifesting isn't always a walk in the park. For many of us, it can be a challenge to believe that what we desire is already ours, especially when our external circumstances seem to tell us otherwise. That's where manifesting techniques come in.

Manifesting techniques, practices, and processes, called "treatments" back in Abdullah's day, help us build belief and stay aligned with assumptions and our core desires. Don't be afraid to experiment. Test them out, see how they make you feel, and pay attention to the results. If a technique feels right and brings you closer to your dreams, keep it. If it doesn't resonate with you, let it go. Like in life, there's no one-size-fits-all in manifesting.

Download your free From Imagination to Reality manifesting kit with additional manifesting processes, affirmations, and more at **FromImaginationtoReality.com**.

The Mental Diet Process

Purpose: To direct our inner conversations.

If one could only control these inner conversations morning, noon, and night, and carry them right into the dream world, he would know what world he is creating. Stop for one moment and ask yourself, what am I thinking now? You are carrying on a little tiny inner speech at every moment of time.

— *Neville*[2]

Do you talk to yourself? I do. Are your self-convos out loud or in your mind? Mine are both.

When you're alone with your thoughts, do you ever notice those little chats you have with yourself? Inner Conversations, a term coined by Neville, are those nonstop dialogues running in our minds throughout the day. These dialogues, filled with beliefs, doubts, hopes, and fears, create scripts that our lives play out to.

Our external world reflects our internal state. If our Inner Conversations are filled with doubt, worry, or fear, our reality will mirror those emotions. On the other hand, if our internal dialogues are positive, encouraging, and confident, our external world will resonate with those vibes. If you are beefing with someone in real life, I guarantee that you're beefing with them in your mind as well.

We've all been there. Those moments when our minds drift into a negativity, doubt, and fear. Just as we choose what we feed our bodies, we have the power to select what we feed our souls and minds.

Imagine your mind as a sacred temple. Every thought you invite in either cleanses, energizes, and adorns the space or clutters and diminishes its divine energy. Now, if you're serious about manifesting your wildest dreams—and I know you are—maintaining this temple is non-negotiable.

Your desires, dreams, and deepest wishes are just waiting for the right signal from you. So, let's clean up the airwaves and tune in to a frequency where miracles aren't just possible, they're inevitable.

A mental diet nurtures your mind—just as you would your body.

The foundation of the mental diet is self-awareness. Become an observer of your own thoughts. Throughout the day, tune in to your inner dialogue. What are the recurring themes? What patterns emerge? Negative thoughts, once identified, need to be halted in their tracks. Use simple tools or mantras as mental stop signs, like "not today" or "I choose differently." Even a simple "stop" can redirect your mental flow.

Seven-Day Mental Diet Challenge

To be done each day:

1. **Daily Check-ins:** Carve out a sacred moment each day, preferably in the morning or before bed, dedicated to introspection. In this quiet space, ask yourself: "What thoughts dominated my day?" This isn't about judgment; it's about awareness. Recognize patterns and acknowledge areas of growth and those that need more nurturing.

2. **Journaling:** Grab a notebook or digital device and dedicate it to this experience. At the end of each day, record the successes you've encountered. Did you stop a negative thought midway? Celebrate it! Also, jot down challenges. Were there particular triggers or situations that made positive alignment tougher? Recognizing these helps in building resilience.

3. **Visualization Practice:** Dedicate a few minutes after your daily check-in for visualization. Close your eyes, take deep breaths, and conjure up images of your desires in their full glory. Don't just see it—immerse yourself in it. Feel the emotions, the excitement, the gratitude of having your desires realized.

4. **Affirmations:** Here's a list of general affirmations to infuse your day with positivity:
   - I am deserving of love, abundance, and success.
   - Every challenge I face is an opportunity for growth.
   - Life conspires in my favor.
   - I am a magnet for positive experiences and fruitful outcomes.
   - With each day, I become a better version of myself.

   Feel free to use these or craft your own. Repeat them throughout the day, especially during challenging moments.

5. **Feedback and Review:** On the seventh day, reflect on the week. Has there been a shift in your mood or feelings? Do certain situations or interactions feel lighter or more harmonious?

> Sometimes, the changes are subtle, like a newfound sense of calm. Other times, there are big shifts in your external circumstances. Both are a testament to your growth and transformation. Happy manifesting!

How to Elevate Inner Conversations

Navigating your inner thoughts might seem tricky at first, but with practice, it gets easier.

- **Tune in to your thoughts.** The first step? Notice what's going on in your head. Take a few quiet moments each day, maybe when you wake up or before you sleep. Listen to the chatter in your mind without judging it.
- **Keep a little notebook with you.** Jot down any big thoughts or feelings that pop up during the day in a thought diary.
- **Hit the stop button on unwanted thoughts.** Caught a thought that feels undesirable? Picture a big, red stop sign in your mind when you want to halt a thought. It's a quick way to change direction. Feeling lost in a thought spiral? Breathe in deeply and then let it out. Do it a few times. It's like a mini break for your mind.
- **Swap the channel.** After stopping a thought you don't like, redirect and find a better one. When an undesired thought comes up, question it. Think, "Is this the whole story?" or "Can I look at this differently?" Then kick out the negative thought and replace it. If you think, "I can't do this," flip it with, "Hey, I've got this!"

The State Akin to Sleep Process

Purpose: To learn to harness your sleep state for manifesting.

The "State Akin to Sleep" is the zone between sleeping and waking when we can most effectively shape our reality. This bridge connects your conscious and subconscious mind. Imagine it as a blank canvas, ready to be filled with your dreams and aspirations.

Your subconscious mind doesn't discern between what's real or imaginary, positive or negative. It just faithfully processes and integrates everything it is fed. When the critical conscious mind is in the driver's seat, it often dismisses or questions our dreams, sabotaging our manifestation process before it even begins. But when we enter the "State Akin to Sleep," the conscious mind falls back, providing a clear pathway to the subconscious.

What to do: The "State Akin to Sleep" as taught by Neville can be considered a form of meditation, but with a specific intention and focus. It's a dance between relaxation and focus. As you prepare for bed, allowing your body to unwind and your mind to slow down, you find yourself hovering at the edge of sleep. This is your golden moment. Instead of fully giving in to the pull of sleep, linger in this in-between realm.

In this state, gently introduce your dreams and desires. Don't just visualize these dreams, but feel them. Feel the joy of your goal achieved. Feel as though what you desire is already a reality. This act of "feeling it real" kickstarts the juicy manifestation process.

Reasons It May Not Be Working

- **Lack of Consistency:** If you're not regularly dedicating time to this practice, it may not manifest the results you hope for. These things take time and consistent nurturing.
- **Disbelief or Doubt:** If deep down, you don't believe that your desires can manifest or that the "State Akin to Sleep" can help, then that disbelief can block your progress. Doubt sends mixed signals, disrupting the clear channel needed for manifestation.
- **Underlying Fear or Anxiety:** Sometimes, underlying fears or anxieties can prevent us from fully embracing and benefiting from this state. If you're afraid of change, or if you're anxious about your goals coming true, these feelings can create a blockage in manifestation.
- **Not Being Specific:** When you're visualizing in the "State Akin to Sleep," be specific about what you want. Vague or ambiguous desires can lead to vague or ambiguous results.
- **Physical Discomfort:** If you're not physically comfortable when you're trying to enter this state—too cold, too warm, or in a noisy environment—this can stop you from relaxing enough to successfully achieve the "State Akin to Sleep."

If you're encountering these challenges, don't beat yourself up. Awareness is the first step. Remind yourself that it's okay to encounter obstacles. They're not roadblocks. They're stepping stones toward your manifestation.

The Revision Process

Purpose: To revise the experiences and memories that are undesired.

Ever wish you could hit the rewind button and change a past event? That's where Neville's idea of "revision" comes in. If your thoughts and feelings shape what comes next, then changing how you see a past event can help you shape a brighter future. Revision isn't about pretending something didn't happen. It's about taking control of your story.

Memories aren't just the past. They're alive in our minds. Every time we think back to a memory, we're not just watching a replay. We can change the story. And when we change that story, we change how we see the world and what we believe is possible.

Imagine you had a tough job interview once. If you always think back to it as a disaster, you'll probably feel nervous for your next one. But if you change that memory and imagine it went really well, you'll approach the next interview feeling like a rock star. It's not just "think happy thoughts." It's "feel and believe in a new story."

Revision, the Transformative Power

Let me tell you about my client "Sarai." Back in high school, she missed a big exam because of a mix-up. She felt this one mistake threw her off track for years. Every time she faced something new, she'd remember that missed exam and think she was bound to mess up again.

But then we did revision together. Instead of being stuck in the past, she changed the memory. She pictured herself taking the exam and doing super well. Over time, this new story helped her feel more confident. The next challenge she faced? She went in thinking, "I've got this!"

Sarai's experience shows us how past memories can shape our present. But by revising them, we can heal and start expecting good things to happen. Even if we can't change what happened, we can change how it makes us feel. By doing that, we can rewrite our future.

1. **Find a quiet, comfortable space.** Find a sanctuary where you feel safe, undisturbed, and at ease.
2. **Relax the mind and body.** Close your eyes. Start with deep, intentional breaths, imagining every inhalation infusing you with calm and every exhalation releasing your worries. Consider playing soft, ambient music.

Recall the Event: Facing the Memory

1. **Select and reflect.** Choose an event from the past that keeps pulling you back. It might be a missed opportunity, an awkward conversation, or a larger life event.
2. **Experience it vividly.** Recall the surroundings—the colors, the ambiance, the people involved. Hear the dialogues and feel the emotions, whether they're subtle stings or overwhelming waves. By fully immersing yourself, you're preparing the canvas for your masterpiece of change.

Reimagine the Event

1. **Modify the event.** Visualize an alternative scenario. What if things had taken a different turn? Maybe you said the right words, took that chance, or stood up for yourself. Imagine these new scenes replacing the old ones, like swapping out scenes in a movie. I like to turn the undesired memory black and white and then watch it fade away.
2. **Involve your senses.** To make this new memory take root deeply, . see the vibrant colors, feel the textures, and hear the sounds. Maybe there's the smell of your favorite candle or the touch of a loving hand. The richer the details, the more tangible the new memory.

Emotional Anchoring: Securing Your New Narrative

Emotions are the glue that bind memories to our consciousness. So, when you're revising a memory, anchor it with powerful, positive emotions so that it becomes the dominant version in our minds.

1. **Surround yourself with positive emotions.** As the scenes of your newly crafted memory play out, dive into the emotions associated with it. Is it the giddy excitement of a win, the calming touch of relief, the soaring feeling of pride, or pure, unfiltered happiness? Each of these emotions has a unique vibe: texture, color, and weight. Welcome them all.
2. **Bask in the radiance.** Allow the positive emotions to envelop you. Visualize the positivity as a golden light, illuminating every corner of

your being, banishing shadows and doubts. (Sounds corny, but it works if you work it!)

Releasing and Letting Go: Embracing the New

The art of revision doesn't end at rewriting a memory. It reaches completion when we can let go of the old version, fully trusting the new narrative we created.

1. **Trust in your power.** Reflect on how many times your thoughts, both conscious and subconscious, have shaped your reality. Feel a deep sense of respect and trust toward this power you hold. Every change you visualize has the potential to create a new path for your life.
2. **Give the difficult memory a grace-filled release.** See the original memory as a paper boat or a fragile balloon. See it in your hands, acknowledge it for its lessons, thank it for its role in your growth, and then gently release it. Feel a sense of lightness, a release of weight. You now hold a more vibrant, empowering memory.

Enhance Revision with the State Akin to Sleep (SATS)

By revising memories in this state, you deliver a direct message to your subconscious. You bypass the usual guards and filters of the conscious mind. This receptive phase makes it a great time to embed new narratives.

As you settle into bed, or even for a nap, use deep and conscious breathing. Transition from the day's hustle and let yourself slip into a relaxed state.

Just as you feel you're on the edge of sleep remain slightly alert, and start your revision process. See the event you want to change, reimagine the outcome, and soak in the feelings of this new version. These feelings are your direct line to the subconscious.

Then, allow yourself to release and sleep. This transition imprints the updated memory.

The Magic of Daily Do-Overs

Have you ever wished you could hit a "redo" button on certain parts of your day? Well, with the magic of daily revision, you kind of can!

Making revision a nightly habit is like doing daily workouts for your mind. Over time, you get stronger, and facing life's challenges becomes a bit easier. Spending a few moments each night to "redo" parts of your day can set you up for a happier tomorrow.

The Sit in the Hall Process

Purpose: To realize all things are possible with astral projection.

Abdullah taught Neville a method for astral projection. The "Sit in the Hall" practice involves a daily visualization exercise during which Neville would sit in his living room and assume or imagine himself sitting at a telephone in the hallway, even though he couldn't physically see it from his seat. He would mentally go back and forth between the two places, getting a feeling of movement.

Neville used this astral projection exercise to strengthen his imagination and loosen the connection to his physical body. With practice, he learned that he could mentally travel to any place he wanted, feeling like he was really there. He even had experiences where other people saw him in the place he was imagining, even though he wasn't physically there.

The key is to shift your thinking from just imagining a place you want to be to actually feeling like you're there. This change in perspective lets you test how well you're projecting by thinking about where familiar people and places would be in relation to where you're imagining yourself.

Practicing regularly will help you master this skill and use the power of assumption to bring positive changes into your life. Neville connects this practice to the idea of prayer, which he defines as moving toward or being close to something you want. He says that the most effective prayer, once you've mastered this technique, is simply saying "Thank you, Father," acknowledging that your prayers are always heard.

Abdullah's teachings emphasize the role of imagination and assumption in shaping our reality. By mentally placing yourself in a desired location or state, you can overcome physical barriers and draw closer to your goals, even if you can't physically be there.

This involves shifting your consciousness to different locations through the power of imagination.

What to do:

1. **Find a quiet and comfortable space.** Choose a spot where you can sit or lie down comfortably, and where you won't be disturbed.
2. **Relax your body.** Take a few deep breaths and allow your body to relax. Let go of any tension or stress in your muscles.
3. **Choose a destination.** Decide on a specific location where you want to project yourself.

It could be anywhere in the world—a familiar place or somewhere you've never been.

4. **Visualize your destination.** Close your eyes and start visualizing the location you've chosen. Picture the surroundings, the sounds, the smells, and the sensations of being there. Imagine it as vividly as possible.
5. **Shift your perspective.** Imagine yourself sitting or standing in your chosen location. At this point, you should shift your perspective from thinking *of* the location to thinking *from* the location. In other words, instead of imagining yourself being there, assume that you are already there.
6. **Test your assumption.** To test whether you've successfully shifted your perspective, think of people or places that are familiar to you in your current physical location. If you're projecting yourself to New York City, for example, think of friends or family who live in your hometown. They should feel distant, as if they are thousands of miles away from where you are now. This indicates that you've made the mental shift.
7. **Move between locations.** Practice shifting your consciousness between your physical location and your chosen destination. Imagine yourself moving back and forth between the two locations. Feel the sensation of changing in motion.
8. **Anchor yourself in the new location.** Focus on your chosen location and anchor yourself there mentally. Make your visualization so strong that you feel as if you are physically present in the new location. Believe that you are there.

9. **Return to your physical body.** When you're ready to end the session, gradually shift your consciousness back to your physical body. Reorient yourself to your physical surroundings and slowly open your eyes.
10. **Practice regularly.** This technique may take time to master. Regular practice will help you improve your ability to shift your consciousness and project yourself to different locations.

The Ladder Experiment Process

Purpose: To prove to yourself the power of your subconscious mind.

Neville's Ladder Experiment is a cool way to see how your imagination can turn into real-life manifestations. Here's how it works: Right before you go to sleep, imagine yourself climbing a ladder. See it and feel it, but tell yourself you're not going to climb a ladder anytime soon, no matter what. Then, keep an eye out to see if a ladder shows up in your life anyway in the next few days.

This experiment of the Law of Life blends Neville's focus on imagination with Murphy's emphasis on the subconscious. If you can picture something in your mind's eye with enough vividness and emotion, it holds the potential to materialize in your external reality. Despite conscious resistance, if the subconscious has embraced a belief, it will work diligently to bring it to fruition.

The Ladder Experiment is a gentle nudge toward challenging our everyday beliefs, revealing the power of even the slightest imaginative act. So, see this experiment as your personal proof lab, a hands-on way to see the teachings of Abdullah come alive.

What to do:

1. **Find a quiet spot.** Doing this exercise right before you go to sleep is best. Make sure you're comfy and relaxed.
2. **See the ladder through your point of view.** Close your eyes and picture yourself climbing a ladder. Don't see it like you're watching a movie of yourself—instead, see it as if you're doing it right now.
3. **Make it real.** Think about how the ladder feels under your hands. Imagine lifting your feet and the little sounds you might hear. The more real it feels, the better.
4. **Say you won't do it.** This might sound funny, but the next day, tell yourself (and even friends or family if you want) that you're not going to climb any ladder. It's a fun twist to the experiment!
5. **Look for ladders in the real world.** For the next few days, just notice what's happening around you. See if ladders pop up in unexpected places or if you are forced to climb one. But don't force it—let things happen naturally. Everyone's experience is different. Some end up climbing a ladder soon, while others take a bit longer. Just enjoy the process and see what you learn about the power of the subconscious mind!

Your Ladder Reflection

Capture each ladder sighting or moment in an old-school journal or your favorite note-taking app. This isn't about climbing that ladder. It's the magic of synchronicity, where your inner beliefs dance with Infinite Intelligence. When that "climbing" moment finds you—be it tomorrow, next week, or beyond—acknowledge it. Ah, the dance of co-creation!

Please find additional resources at
FromImaginationToReality.com
and Womanifesting.com.

Find me on social media at @abiolaTV.

ENDNOTES

INTRODUCTION

1. Neville Goddard, *At Your Command: Embracing 'I AM': Your Gateway to God Consciousness and Limitless Potential,* (Watchmaker Publishing: 2015)

2. Max Herrick Shenk, "How Abdullah Taught Neville the Law: 'He turned his back on me and … slammed the door!'," *Max Herrick Shenk, Writer* (blog), last modified March 24, 2017, https://maxharrickshenk.wordpress.com/2017/03/24/how-abdullah-taught-neville-the-law-he-turned-his-back-on-me-and-slammed-the-door.

3. Neville Goddard, *The Power of Awareness:* (TarcherPerigree: 2012)

4. "'About Abdullah' Neville Goddard Research (New York) Part #1," *Cool Wisdom Books* (blog), accessed November 4, 2023, https://coolwisdombooks.com/about-abdullah-neville-goddard-research-new-york.

5. "Neville Goddard: A Portrait by Israel Regardie," *Cool Wisdom Books* (blog), accessed November 4, 2023, https://coolwisdombooks.com/neville/neville-goddard-a-portrait-by-israel-regardie.

6. "Sacred African Science and Beyond: Abdullah's Influence on Neville Goddard's Law of Assumption," *Digital Journal* (press release), June 23, 2023, https://www.digitaljournal.com/pr/news/getnews/sacred-african-science-and-beyond-abdullah-s-influence-on-neville-goddard-s-law-of-assumption#ixzz8C1hdcOcU.

7. "Neville the Ultimate Businessman—Debunking the Myth NEVILLE DIDN'T CHARGE MONEY!" Neville Goddard Next Generation, December 19, 2022, YouTube video, https://www.youtube.com/watch?v=gZjisNyzUXI.

8. "Neville Goddard Lectures: 'The Supreme Ideal'," *Cool Wisdom Books* (blog), accessed November 23, 2023, https://coolwisdombooks.com/neville/neville-goddard-lectures-the-supreme-ideal.

PART I

1. Neville Goddard, *At Your Command: Embracing 'I AM': Your Gateway to God Consciousness and Limitless Potential*, (Watchmaker Publishing: 2015)
2. "Neville Goddard: 'Thinking Fourth Dimensionally' – Lesson #3," *Cool Wisdom Books* (blog), accessed November 2, 2023, https://coolwisdombooks.com/neville/neville-goddard-thinking-fourth-dimensionally-lesson-3.
3. "Neville Goddard: The Miracle of Imagination by Margaret Ruth Broome," *Cool Wisdom Books* (blog), accessed November 2, 2023, https://coolwisdombooks.com/neville/nevillegoddard-the-miracle-of-imagination-by-margaret-ruth-broome.
4. Neville Goddard, *The Power of Awareness*: (TarcherPerigree: 2012)
5. "You are in Barbados! How Abdullah Taught Neville Goddard the Law," Giancarlo Serra (blog), accessed November 2, 2023, https://www.giancarloserra.org/you-are-in-barbados-how-abdullah-taught-neville-goddard-the-law.
6. "Neville Goddard: 'Thinking Fourth Dimensionally' – Lesson #3," *Cool Wisdom Books* (blog), accessed November 2, 2023, https://coolwisdombooks.com/neville/neville-goddard-thinking-fourth-dimensionally-lesson-3.
7. "THE IMMORTAL MAN: A Treasury of Inspiration and Spiritual Comfort by One of America's Great New Thought Teachers" https://www.youtube.com/watch?v=wczjuBkv7FQ

PART III

1. Neville Goddard, "Changing the Feeling of 'I' (1953)," Neville Goddard Audio and Text Archive, accessed November 2, 2023, https://realneville.com/txt/changing_the_feeling_of_i.htm.
2. Neville Goddard The Only God Is I Am" Brian Scott, May 29, 2023, YouTube video, https://www.youtube.com/watch?v=o_Z2IF4iuzk.
3. Neville Goddard, "I Am All Imagination (June 4 1971)," *Free Neville* (blog), accessed November 2, 2023, https://freeneville.com/i-am-all-imagination-june-4-1971-free-

neville-goddard-pdf/. Neville Goddard, “Gifts Bestowed by God (1971),” https://archive.org/stream/NevilleGoddard001/gifts_bestowed_by_god_djvu.txt.

4. Kristin Ashbacher et al., “Good Stress, Bad Stress, and Oxidative Stress: Insights from Anticipatory Cortisol Reactivity,” *Psychoneuroendocrinology* 38, no. 9 (2013): 1698–1708, https://doi.org/10.1016/j.psyneuen.2013.02.004.

5. Stéphane Doyen et al., “Behavioral Priming: It's All in the Mind, But Whose Mind?,” *PloS one* 7, no. 1 (2012): e29081, https://doi.org/10.1371/journal.pone.0029081.

6. Neville Goddard, “Changing the Feeling of 'I',” Neville Goddard Audio and Text Archive, accessed November 4, 2023, https://realneville.com/txt/changing_the_feeling_of_i.htm.

7. Neville Goddard: “'Thinking Fourth Dimensionally' – Lesson #3,” *Cool Wisdom Books* (blog), accessed November 2, 2023, https://coolwisdombooks.com/neville/neville-goddard-thinking-fourth-dimensionally-lesson-3.

8. Neville Goddard, *Your Faith Is Your Fortune.*

9. Neville Goddard Lectures: 'I AM in You' (1968),” *Cool Wisdom Books* (blog), accessed November 2, 2023, https://coolwisdombooks.com/neville/i-am-in-you.

10. https://www.oprah.com/oprahs-lifeclass/jill-bolte-taylors-stroke-of-insight-video

11. https://www.hintsa.com/insights/blogs/improve-your-emotional-self-awareness/#:~:text=Dr.,stay%20in%20that%20emotional%20loop.%E2%80%9D

12. “Neville Goddard Lectures: 'The One Greater Than John' – The 1964 Lectures,” *Cool Wisdom Books* (blog), accessed November 2, 2023, https://coolwisdombooks.com/neville/neville-goddard-the-one-greater-than-john-the-1964-lectures.

13. "Neville Goddard Lectures: 'In Praise of Wisdom' (1965)," *Cool Wisdom Books* (blogs), accessed November 2, 2023, https://coolwisdombooks.com/neville/neville-goddard-lectures-in-praise-of-wisdom.

14. “Neville Goddard Research: Rev. Frederick Eikerenkoetter, Jr. (Rev. Ike) and Neville Goddard,” *Cool Wisdom Books* (blog), accessed November 2, 2023, https://coolwisdombooks.com/neville-goddard-research-rev-frederick-eikerenkoetter-jr-rev-ike-and-neville-goddard.

15. "United Palace (Formerly Loew's 175th Street Theatre," Landmarks Preservation Commission, Designation List 492 LP-0656, December 13, 2016, http://s-media.nyc.gov/agencies/lpc/lp/0656.pdf.

16. Frederick Eikerenkoetter, *Rev. Ike's Secrets For Health, Joy and Prosperity, For YOU: A Science Of Living Study Guide* ((Independently published: 1982).

17. Clayton Riley, "The Golden Gospel of Reverend Ike," *New York Times*, March 9, 1975, https://www.nytimes.com/1975/03/09/archives/the-golden-gospel-of-reverend-ike-revike.html.

18. Frederick Eikerenkoetter, *Rev. Ike's Secrets For Health, Joy and Prosperity, For YOU: A Science Of Living Study Guide* ((Independently published: 1982).

19. "Neville Goddard Quotes," New Neville Goddard Quotes Daily, https://nevillegoddardquotes.com/you-are-the-power-neville-goddard-quotes/.

20. Neville Goddard, "The First Principle (1969)," Neville Goddard Audio and Text Archive, ttps://realneville.com/txt/the_first_principle.htm.

21. Dr. Daniel Banks, Say Word! Voices from Hip Hop Theater (Ann Arbor: University of Michigan Press, 2011).

22. "Neville Goddard Lectures: 'In Praise of Wisdom' (1965)," *Cool Wisdom Books* (blog), accessed November 2, 2023, https://coolwisdombooks.com/neville/neville-goddard-lectures-in-praise-of-wisdom.

23. "Neville Goddard: A Portrait by Israel Regardie," *Cool Wisdom Books* (blog), accessed November 2, 2023, https://coolwisdombooks.com/neville/neville-goddard-a-portrait-by-israel-regardie.

24. Neville Goddard Lectures: "The Cabala" Jan 15, 1965 https://coolwisdombooks.com/neville/neville-goddard-the-cabala

25. Rev. Ike Legacy, 2023, "A Rev. Ike Affirmative Prayer," Facebook, March 23, 2023, https://www.facebook.com/photo.php?fbid=799296081560787&id=100044412072092&set=a.203577554465979.

26. "Neville Goddard Lectures: 'The Cabala' (1965)," *Cool Wisdom Books* (blog), accessed November 2, 2023, https://coolwisdombooks.com/neville/neville-goddard-the-cabala.

27. Louise L. Hay, *Mirror Work: 21 Days to Heal Your Life* (Carlsbad, CA: Hay House, Inc., 2016).

28. "How Neville Goddard Manifested His Wife in One Week," *Giancarlo Serra* (blog), accessed November 2, 2023, https://www.giancarloserra.org/how-neville-goddard-manifested-his-wife-in-one-week.

29. "Neville Goddard Lectures: 'Who Are the Condemned?' (1964)," *Cool Wisdom Books* (blog), accessed November 2, 2023, https://coolwisdombooks.com/neville/neville-goddard-who-are-the-condemned.

30. Neville Goddard, "I Am All Imagination – June 4 1971," *Free Neville* (blog), accessed November 2, 2023, https://freeneville.com/i-am-all-imagination-june-4-1971-free-neville-goddard-pdf/.

31. "Neville Goddard Lectures: 'The Congregation of God' (1966)," *Cool Wisdom Books* (blog), accessed November 2, 2023, https://coolwisdombooks.com/neville/neville-goddard-lectures-the-congregation-of-god-1966.

32. "Neville Goddard Lectures: 'The Supreme Ideal' (1964)," *Cool Wisdom Books* (blog), accessed November 2, 2023, https://coolwisdombooks.com/neville/neville-goddard-lectures-the-supreme-ideal.

33. Neville Goddard-How Abdullah Taught The Law (Neville's Teacher)" Neville & The Law, January 24, 2014, YouTube video, https://www.youtube.com/watch?v=3L6B1eGrFvw

34. "Neville Goddard Lectures: 'Abdullah: How We Got Together Q&A'," *Cool Wisdom Books* (blog), accessed November 2, 2023, https://coolwisdombooks.com/neville/neville-goddard-lecture-abdullah-how-we-got-together-qa.

35. "Neville's Teacher Abdullah—#1," *Free Neville* (blog), accessed November 2, 2023, https://freeneville.com/nevilles-teacher-abdulah-asks-are-quibbles-holding-you-back-free-neville-goddard.

36. "Neville Goddard: 'Thinking Fourth Dimensionally' – Lesson #3," *Cool Wisdom Books* (blog), accessed November 2, 2023, https://coolwisdombooks.com/neville/neville-goddard-thinking-fourth-dimensionally-lesson-3.

37. "Neville Goddard Lectures: 'The One Greater Than John' – The 1964 Lectures," *Cool Wisdom Books* (blog), accessed November 2, 2023, https://coolwisdombooks.com/neville/neville-goddard-the-one-greater-than-john-the-1964-lectures.

38. Ibid.

39. "Neville Goddard Lectures: 'The One Greater Than John' – The 1964 Lectures," *Cool Wisdom Books* (blog), accessed

November 2, 2023, https://coolwisdombooks.com/neville/neville-goddard-the-one-greater-than-john-the-1964-lectures.

40. "Neville Goddard: A Portrait by Israel Regardie," *Cool Wisdom Books* (blog), accessed November 2, 2023, https://coolwisdombooks.com/neville/neville-goddard-a-portrait-by-israel-regardie/. Israel Regardie, *The Romance of Metaphysics* (Chicago: Aries Press, 1946).

41. "Neville Goddard Lectures: 'Incubate the Dream' (1963)," *Cool Wisdom Books* (blog), accessed November 2, 2023, https://coolwisdombooks.com/neville/neville-goddard-lectures-incubate-the-dream.

42. "Transcript of 'Freedom On The Beach' Lecture Presented by Freedom Barry Held at Cambria, CA, on Sept. 14–15, 1996," *Cool Wisdom Books* (blog), accessed November 2, 2023, https://coolwisdombooks.com/freedom-on-the-beach-lecture.

43. "Neville Goddard: A Portrait by Israel Regardie," *Cool Wisdom Books* (blog), accessed November 4, 2023, https://coolwisdombooks.com/neville/neville-goddard-a-portrait-by-israel-regardie.

44. "Neville Goddard Lectures: 'Who Are the Condemned?' (1964)," *Cool Wisdom Books* (blog), accessed November 2, 2023, https://coolwisdombooks.com/neville/neville-goddard-who-are-the-condemned.

45. "There Are No 'Ascended Masters' – Neville Goddard on Baird T. Spalding," *Cool Wisdom Books* (blog), accessed November 2, 2023, https://coolwisdombooks.com/neville/there-are-no-ascended-masters-neville-goddard-on-baird-t-spalding.

46. "Neville Goddard Lectures: 'Who Are the Condemned?' (1964)," *Cool Wisdom Books* (blog), accessed November 2, 2023, https://coolwisdombooks.com/neville/neville-goddard-who-are-the-condemned.

BONUS

1. "Neville Goddard: 'Thinking Fourth Dimensionally' – Lesson #3," *Cool Wisdom Books* (blog), accessed November 2, 2023, https://coolwisdombooks.com/neville/neville-goddard-thinking-fourth-dimensionally-lesson-3.

2. "Neville Goddard Lectures: 'Control Your Inner Conversations Mind' (1971)," *Cool Wisdom Books* (blog), accessed November 2, 2023, https://coolwisdombooks.com/neville/control-your-inner-conversations.

ACKNOWLEDGMENTS

Great Ancestor Abdullah, thank you for being a guiding star for all of us seeking to consciously live our wildest dreams and manifest our truest selves. Your teachings have put me on a path where my deepest aspirations meet reality.

To Great Ancestors Neville Goddard, Joseph Murphy, Reverend Ike, Dr. Wayne Dyer, Louise Hay and all the brilliant minds who knowingly or unknowingly shared teachings rooted in Abdullah's well of wisdom, thank you!

My dear reader, receiving Abdullah's wisdom has been a transformative experience of alchemy, personal power and enlightenment that I wish to share with you. This work continues my mission of Sankofa, recovering ancestral knowledge and magic for us and the generations to come. We are Abdullah's legacy. For my Manifest Your Magic and Womanifesting Circles, Spiritpreneur students, Goddess Temple podcast audience, Priestess of Power retreat alums, this is a tribute to each of you. My hope is that this book serves as a catalyst for awakening the power within you, inspiring self-discovery, transformation, and co-creation.

To Norma, Ovid, Ovid Jr., Damali Abrams, Michelle Gaul, Adana Collins, and my entire beloved family—and my cherished friends—my heart overflows with gratitude for your unwavering support and love. In the past year my life shifts included: moving countries, being a new mommy, and buying a home, and I couldn't have done any of that if you didn't have my back. My jewel, Amethyst-Ruby, thank you for making me laugh and always bringing your mommy back to earth.

Thank you to New Thought scholar and human library Steve Mohammed for sending me down this magical path. And deepest gratitude to all who have preserved these teachings over time and share and discuss it on sites from the r/NevilleGoddard subreddit and Facebook to YouTube and Instagram. Thank you especially to researchers and authors Mitch Horowitz, Max Harrick Shenk, and Tima Vlasto, creator of CoolWisdomBooks.com and Mr. Twenty Twenty and Victoria, founders of FreeNeville.com. Each one, teach one.

Patty Gift at Hay House, thank you for immediately understanding and supporting this important project. You are a wayshower. Goddess Melody Guy, you are a literary lighthouse, always providing direction in creative storms. Reid Tracey and the rest of my Hay House team—thank you! Each of you has played a vital role in ensuring that Abdullah's work reaches our beautiful audience.

I am filled with gratitude and humility.

ABOUT THE AUTHOR

Abiola Abrams is an intuitive self-worth coach, popular keynote speaker, award-winning author, international retreat leader, columnist, and media personality who empowers Big Vision Women to find freedom from their personal fears, manifest authentic power, and align with purpose.

The founder of Mawu's Goddess Mystery School and the international Goddess Retreats, Abiola is the author of the acclaimed *African Goddess Initiation: Sacred Rituals for Self-Love, Prosperity and Joy,* best-selling *African Goddess Rising,* and *Secrets of the Ancestors Oracle.* Her most recent meditation album is called "Enter the Goddess Temple."

In addition to Abiola's popular online group coaching programs and courses, Abiola has given motivational advice on networks from the CW, BET, and Discovery Channel to MTV and the BBC as well as sites and publications from the DailyOm and Huffington Post to Match.com and *Essence Magazine.*

Abiola also leads transformational workshops and speaks at universities, corporations, and organizations from Microsoft and Dropbox to Cornell University, and creates global spiritual wellness retreats from Bali to Belize. In addition, Abiola is on the faculty of leading wellness and personal development organizations such as The

Omega Institute for Holistic Studies, The Shift Network, Hay House's I Can Do It Summit, and London's College of Psychic Studies.

Along with a bachelor's degree in sociology and creative writing from Sarah Lawrence, and master's degree from Vermont College of Fine Arts in women's media and storytelling, Abiola's coaching certifications include neuro-linguistic programming from American Union of NLP. Her practice includes teachings in mindfulness, emotional freedom technique, and intuitive mindset reprogramming. Abiola's first book, *Dare,* was published by Simon and Schuster, while her book *The Sacred Bombshell Handbook of Self-Love* was the winner of an African American Literary Award for Best Self-Help.

Abiola started out as a lifestyle journalist, popular columnist, documentarian, and TV presenter.

As the first person in her family born in America, Abiola is passionate about midwifing conscious women leaders to breakthrough and is committed to using her gifts to inspire, uplift, and transform.

To learn more about Abiola and her work, visit: **womanifesting.com**, and find free resources for this book at **FromImaginationToReality.com**.

Hay House Titles of Related Interest

YOU CAN HEAL YOUR LIFE, the movie,
starring Louise Hay & Friends
(available as an online streaming video)
www.hayhouse.com/louise-movie

THE SHIFT, the movie,
starring Dr. Wayne W. Dyer
(available as an online streaming video)
www.hayhouse.com/the-shift-movie

❖ ❖ ❖

ANCESTORS SAID:
365 Introspections for Emotional Healing,
by Ehime Ora

BECOMING SUPERNATURAL:
How Common People Are Doing the Uncommon,
by Dr. Joe Dispenza

BLACK MOON LILITH RISING:
How to Unlock the Power of the Dark Divine Feminine Through Astrology, by Adama Sesay

SPIRITUAL ACTIVATOR:
5 Steps to Clearing, Unblocking, and Protecting Your Energy to Attract More Love, Joy, and Purpose, by Oliver Niño

THE UNIVERSE HAS YOUR BACK:
Transform Fear to Faith, by Gabrielle Bernstein

All of the above are available at your local bookstore, or may be ordered by contacting Hay House (see next page).

❖ ❖ ❖

We hope you enjoyed this Hay House book. If you'd like to receive our online catalog featuring additional information on Hay House books and products, or if you'd like to find out more about the Hay Foundation, please contact:

Hay House Publishers (India) Pvt Ltd
Muskaan Complex, Plot No. 3,
B-2, Vasant Kunj, New Delhi 110 070
Phone: +91 11 41761620
www.hayhouse.co.in

—

Published in the United States by:
Hay House LLC, P.O. Box 5100, Carlsbad, CA 92018-5100
(760) 31-7695 or (800) 654-5126
www.hayhouse.com® • www.hayfoundation.org

Published in Australia by:
Hay House Australia Publishing Pty Ltd
18/36 Ralph St., Alexandria NSW 2015
Phone: +61 (02) 9669 4299
www.hayhouse.com.au

Published in the United Kingdom by:
Hay House UK Ltd
1st Floor, Crawford Corner,
91–93 Baker Street, London W1U 6QQ
Phone: +44 (0)20 3927 7290
www.hayhouse.co.uk

—